IN THE LAND OF DRAGONS

MITALI CHAKRAVARTY

PARTRIDGE

Copyright © 2014 by Mitali Chakravarty.

Library of Congress Control Number:		2014902383
ISBN:	Hardcover	978-1-4907-0434-0
	Softcover	978-1-4907-0433-3
	eBook	978-1-4907-0435-7

Cover Design by Arjo Chakravarty

Print information available on the last page.

To order additional copies of this book, contact
Toll Free 800 101 2657 (Singapore)
Toll Free 1 800 81 7340 (Malaysia)
orders.singapore@partridgepublishing.com

www.partridgepublishing.com/singapore

ACKNOWLEDGEMENTS

I would like to thank my two sons, Arjo and Shourjo, and husband without who this book would not have existed.

I would like to thank my two friends, Erica and Shazia. Erica suggested I put my scrap pieces of writing together and make a book and Shazia read the book before I sent it to the publisher and suggested improvements.

I would like to thank Arsalan for his candid feedback.
I would like to thank all the people who inspired me to write.

Thank you.
Mitali Chakravarty

CONTENTS

PROLOGUE

WHEN I TURNED FORTY, we took a momentous leap in our lives. We moved to China.

China was like no country that I had ever visited or lived in. And I had lived in five countries and visited over a dozen. We have been assigned from Singapore to China. We are Indians who have not lived in our own country for more than twenty years. We are in the process of evolving as citizens of the world.

In China, on one side were the locals, with their distinct culture and history, its roots in the Zhou dynasty dating to 1800 BCE. On the other were a heterogeneous mix of people from all over the world. We belonged to the second category. The great thing about China is that it accepted all of us as people from outside the realm of China, and in that sense unified us into one group: *laowai*, or foreigners. To this day, gates that remain closed to local Chinese open with a smile for a *laowai*.

Of late there are some pockets of "educated" youngsters who suffer from xenophobia and are nasty and mean to foreigners. However, in most countries, we do have people who resent foreigners. I don't think we should judge the population by a minority of nasty people.

When I came to China in 2006, we were still a novelty, and the local population followed us with immense curiosity. Now they take us more for granted because the population of outsiders is on the rise, especially after the rest of the world was hit by the grand recession of 2009.

One of the most challenging aspects of getting along in China is that if you do not know the language, you will end up feeling handicapped. Mind you, if you go to a school to learn Mandarin, you still do not get to communicate with a large part of the population, as they use dialects. I learnt to speak poor Mandarin from my home help and driver. I found warmth and friendliness in the hearts of the local population. I knew they profited from our pockets, but where do you find people servicing you from purely altruistic motives?

The great thing about the Chinese is that they accept you for what you are, interact with you smilingly at their own pace, and, despite all, still maintain their cultural integrity.

Living in China has been an enriching and maturing experience for me. It has helped me step out of clichéd beliefs and to experience the world for myself, for China does contain a microcosm of all the countries in their expat community. It has helped me see how we all are the same despite our so-called national barriers. We all walked out of Africa, developed our distinctive cultures, and met again in China after many centuries to find we have the same concerns underlying our superficial differences.

Living in China has reinforced my belief in a one-world community and a society that is free from all barriers of colour, creed, and race.

My children got an enriching education and an exposure to a variety of cultures, including others in addition to Chinese. They learnt about tolerance and perfection and to dream big things given all the circumstances. All our experiences were uniquely indigenous to China.

I would like to share the fun we have had bringing up children and savouring this mysterious country—so different from any other I had experienced before.

CHAPTER 1

Globalization in Our Backyard

Flowers were blooming, birds were chirping, and spring was hauling itself over the backs of the bleak winter months.

Surya, Jonas, and Henry were hacking rocks in the back garden with hammers. Not that they had been asked to, but they felt the need to. These were three young men from three parts of the world: India-Singapore, Finland, and England, who were unified by their common need to explore a typical Chinese garden. This could happen only in the backyard of an expat household in China, as like the adults, the children also interact with friends from many cultures and countries. We all get bunched together by our distinct differences from the Chinese, both culturally and physically. Our Chinese landlord had the garden landscaped by a professional company before renting us the house. They made rock structures in the garden, which did not exactly entice me to rent the house. Now that we live in the house, Surya, my younger son, and his friends use the garden. We use it for more mundane things, too, like barbecues, sunbathing, and relaxing. Surya and his friends use it to live through their sense of adventure and wonder at the opportunities provided by Chinese landscapers, who created a garden keeping adults, or rather emperors, in mind.

China's one-child policy has made the child not only precious but overprotected. So instead of leaving children to play in the garden, an affluent Chinese family would give a child an entourage of maids, grandparents, and other adults, who constantly watch over the youngster. There is no need to provide a safe play area for a lone child. A group of unattended children like Surya, Jonas, and Henry is unthinkable in the Chinese context. These boys were a group of merry seven-year-olds who had many adventures rediscovering the world on their own.

Then there is a fish pond, which we tried to contract to a professional company for maintenance. They came. They saw. They drained. They put the two surviving fish in a bucket and promised to come with fresh fish and reinstate the old ones in the pond after two days. The fish disappeared the next day from the bucket. We are guessing the birds made a good breakfast of the two-inch red fish. In China, concepts of time are fluid. Less-schooled adults who run such businesses have the same understanding of time as kindergarteners who mix up the different days and weeks and months. After more than three weeks, we gave up all hope of the fish company coming back. We had a dry fish pond, which the boys used like a dry ditch for some time.

Surya wanted to breed tadpoles and frogs in it. My sons started out as city dwellers from Singapore, and they ended up fascinated with what a Chinese garden in China has to offer—frogs or mushrooms, snails or fish ponds. During the tadpole season, despite Surya's pleas, the pond was not opened to frogs and their families. He had to maintain his tadpoles in a high-rimmed plastic plate, which we placed on a stone and concrete table in the garden. The table was put there for people to sit around, while gazing at the fish pond, sipping endless cups of green tea from Chinese teacups, and thinking profound things. However, we let the tadpoles swim in the 'platarium' on the tea table, and then Surya saw them hop away as frogs. Some were left when we went on home leave to Singapore. So Surya, who has learnt to speak Chinese fluently, like his elder brother, Aditya, asked the old Chinese man who waters our garden to fill up the 'platarium' daily. He was a bit disappointed when we returned from our three-week holiday to find that the 'platarium' had disappeared. We told him the tadpoles grew up and hopped into the garden. Therefore, the old man disposed off the plate. We drew no straight answers from the old man, who was much like a kindergartener when it came to accountability.

Then there was a major typhoon. The pond drain got clogged with leaves, and the empty pond filled up with rainwater. It was after this incident that we decided to try keeping fish in the pond by ourselves. In two days, it rained enough for two months, the weather report said. I had never experienced such weather in my life! My boys went out in the rain to check the garden, and Surya was dancing with delight, saying, "The frogs have come back to me. They really like me." There were a number of small frogs in the pond, and Surya was convinced they were the ones that had grown up in his 'platarium'.

One year Surya had the distinction of catching tadpoles with his bare hands, along with some frog eggs, which he professed hatched into more tadpoles! In fact, he had become the best tadpole catcher in the neighbourhood. A security guard from our compound trained him. The security guards enjoyed boyish preoccupations, including training young men to become expert tadpole catchers, and sometimes I have seen them even teasing or playing with the young boys. In Singapore, the security guards in our compound hardly interact with children, and frogs near the fountains, swimming pool, or play area would probably draw wails of protests from mothers. That spring, Surya gave the tadpoles his own concoctions of plants mixed with dirty water, and they seem to be doing well. The ones that were the size of five-mao coins looked menacing to me. Jonas saved the tadpoles from the wicked cat by covering their jar with a basket.

And then, Surya had this little frog that lived in the fishpond. So, in a way, he did have a pet frog. I would not want it any closer than the pond!

The summer Aditya was thirteen and Surya was five, I was actually cooking for tadpoles.

Aditya's romance with frogs started in kindergarten in Singapore, when his classmate got a frog pet for show-and-tell from the "wild grassland behind his home". They were five years old.

And Aditya fell in love with frogs. He, of course, as befits all macho men of his age, did not like the story of Frog Prince. For that matter, he confided in me he did not even like the story of Beauty and the Beast, as the monster turned into a handsome prince. He did not like princesses either.

I didn't like the idea of a frog pet, as I thought of the slimy creature hopping all over and maybe even sitting in my favourite seat and croaking on my bed . . . or worse, maybe, dancing in my coffee mug or wanting to share the dinner on my plate with me. Then I would need to clean its droppings, as I had to for the indoor fish. In the days of yore, I had to go through the torture of cleaning the stinky fish-tank water. Then the task was taken over by my husband and Aditya as a form of relaxation, though how anybody could relax handling stinky, dirty fish-poo water is beyond my understanding! Nowadays, Aditya feeds the fish in the fish pond and supervises the cleaning crew of our pond, which is basically the old man who waters my garden. In China, it is easy to get local help for the garden if you pay some extra money, unlike in Singapore, where rules about employing anyone are much more stringent.

Surya missed his tadpoles so much after returning from Singapore that he picked up fish that look a bit like tadpoles for our indoor fish tank. We found one of the pair dead after a day. Aditya researched on the Net and found we had bought some variety of miniature freshwater puffer fish. These are extremely hard to care for, and they do not like fish food in jars. They need to be fed worms and snails! Well, I bought a jar of cat food with shrimp, as I could not find jars of worms or snails in the fish-food area of the supermarket. So, the second fish was separated. Aditya put salt in its tank. A worm from our garden and a shrimp from the can lay untouched in its separate home. Maybe cat food was not the puffer fish's cup of tea. After a couple of days, the second fish died too. And these rare fish were being sold as freshwater fish in a jar in the local pet and flower market. The shopkeeper told us they survived in plain tap water! This would be unimaginable in Singapore.

One of Aditya's classmates had bought a pet tarantula from the same pet market. You can find vendors of such stuff sitting with cages and bowls of strange pets, including a variety of weird bugs and venomous snakes, on the sidewalks of the flower and pet market. I have never seen such a strange assortment of pets anywhere else in the world. We all got to hear of the tarantula when the family moved back to their home country and the boy was looking for a home for his pet. My doors were closed to a pet tarantula, as were most other moms' doors. I do not know what happened to it in the end.

Surya has also requested for a wall-climbing common lizard as a pet when we return to Singapore. He has an antarium now. There are five huge, black ants in a plastic case filled with blue gel. The blue gel is agar, I think. This was a Christmas present from one of his friends. We feed them icing sugar every day through a tiny hole.

I have fed them all—boys, ants, tadpoles, fish, men, women, girls, babies, etc, etc, etc. When I spotted a mouse or rat in my kitchen, again an occurrence which I had never faced in my Singapore flat, Surya wanted that as a pet too! Everybody except me was entertained by the rodent in my house. I saw it and heard it, and then it disappeared. It was near my kitchen trash can and making bizarre clicking sounds. I googled it later. It seems they make that sound when they are happy or they eat. Maybe this one was happily eating some kitchen trash! Now I have fed a rat or mouse too . . . though unintentionally.

Anyway, I was terrified when I glimpsed the rat. I shouted for my *ayi* (home help) in absolute distress and said in Chinese that there was a *lao hu* (tiger) in the house. I was so horrified that I had mixed up the words *lao shu* (rat) with *lao hu*. Instead of understanding my terror, my help and my family of three could not stop laughing. One good thing about China is that your ayi has no sense of class barriers and is therefore friendly by nature. Of course, the disadvantage is that you need to make sure she does all the work without hurting her. If you upset a worker or an ayi, chances are they will just stop coming without pre-informing you, and your work will remain undone, even if they go unpaid.

I was finally driven in desperation to inform my house agent. He promptly bought me rat traps. As I found the young gentleman coughing and recovering from a cold, and it was two degrees outside, I asked my driver to take him to the shops to buy the mousetraps. Our driver, a twenty-seven-year-old Chinese who can speak English, could not stop smiling. He kept asking for details of the mouse and grinning. Finally I told him, "Do not look so happy. I am terrified of mice and rats."

My rat saga has yet to reach a conclusion. The rat does not seem to come near the trap or our home anymore. Meanwhile, one of my neighbours has been battling a rat for many days. It looks like after her kids go to sleep, the rodent comes to visit them in their parlour. It scampers across the carpet and sits next to my neighbour on the sofa. When I told my house agent our stories, he said he would also organize pest control experts for our home and the neighbourhood.

I look forward to the day when my home and neighbourhood is free of all rodents again. Till now, the rodent elimination experts seem to be mythical. Again, I remind myself, I do not have access to an edition of yellow pages in China, and agents can do so much and no more, as they have to deal with the same army of workers who are much like children who need to be alternately reprimanded and petted.

Moving from rodents to reptiles . . . when Surya was about one, Aditya had a pet turtle. When we put it on the table, it ran! We had to chase it, capture it, and put it back in its tank.

When we came for our look-see trip from Singapore to Suzhou, China, the turtle developed a lump. My home help had hassles babysitting the turtle. Aditya was sad. But as we had to go to Suzhou within a couple of months, we persuaded Aditya to let it go.

I personally feel it is best to let creatures live in nature, undisturbed by human attention. They were not put on earth for our amusement.

I don't like animals, but animals seem to like me, especially dogs. Our friends' dogs like to wag their tails, smell me, and especially sit under my chair. One of the dogs even took to poking me with his nose from under my patio chair.

The worst was when I agreed to babysit a neighbour's four-year-old twins. Their three-year-old brother had injured his head and had to be rushed to the doctor at night. So when Anne called me for help, I just rushed to the flat. Anne is a Brazilian married to an American Chinese who is more American than most Americans I have met. His father evidently swam the oceans, literally, to set up home in the USA more than half a century ago. They have come back now. Such mixed families are a common occurrence in Suzhou. You have Finns married to Chileans—from two distant corners of the world—Thais married to Germans; Norwegian, Americans, and Croatians married to French; French married to Germans; Chinese locals married to Indians, Pakistanis, German, French, and Polish . . . any country imaginable. Most of them fall into the foreigner category. Sometimes the Chinese women married to foreigners form links between the two communities.

In Anne's case, her husband needed to adjust to the new China, and they definitely fell into the foreigners' category. In Suzhou, most foreigners become like extended family for each other, as they have no physical access to their own families. So we look out for each other when we are in need. When I agreed to babysit, what I overlooked was Anne's little lapdog. He tried to lick me. I don't like being licked. The little boys offered to lock him up. I said there was no need, because I felt they needed to have the comfort of having their pet around while their parents were away with their baby brother in the hospital. Eventually, I managed to persuade the boys to go to bed when I told them their pet seemed sleepy. The pet's bed was in the boys' room. After I turned off the lights for them, the dog started barking. A little voice told me, "You have to let the dog out when he barks." So I did, and then the dog turned crazy! He ran up and down, with and without a toy in his mouth—the whole length of the hall, and then he went toward the back of the kitchen. He was growling and trying to tear the toy while running. Finally I called up Anne to ask her what to do. She said that she was on the way home—all done—and her dog was probably missing her! After that, I explained to the dog that we each had our boundaries. He could not lick me, and I would not cuddle him. And I told him that the boys would wake up if he kept barking, and that Anne was on her way back. The dog seemed to understand what I said. He went quietly to the room and ran out when Anne returned with her son and husband to welcome them back, as did the twin who was awake. But I do know dog-sitting is not an experience I want to relive!

Each day, Surya begs me for a pet, ranging from an elephant to a dog. Well, we do have pets—fish. Perhaps that is why he has now resorted to begging for more frogs and lizards!

I develop a weird kind of attachment to pets. I feel sorry for them and take care of them so that they are not unhappy or discomfited. In return, they become more affectionate toward me than I like, as did Brownie, Anne's dog.

The worst was when Aditya's frog dream came true. He was twelve then and had me cook for his pets, as I mentioned earlier.

What happened was one spring in Suzhou there were, as usual, swarms of tadpoles in the stream in front of our second house. The fish pond house is the fourth one in my housing saga in China. It is a good idea, in my experience, to move every few years in Suzhou, since the houses fall into disrepair within a short span. This time the children did some serious fishing, and we were richer by six tadpoles. Aditya was very happy. He said, "At last we have frog pets." Surya wanted to keep them indoors. We battled to keep them on the patio table. We won the first battle.

Aditya, who is really computer savvy, checked the Internet for what the tadpoles eat. He told me I would have to boil lettuce for ten minutes every day for the tadpoles. So I did for five weeks. And not just that . . . I cleaned the tadpole jar. My ayi grumbled. Most ayis are not too fond of pets, I found. My husband said that the grown-up frogs would adore me and never leave our patio. I was really terrified of being in the frog princess's predicament. So, after five weeks of boiling lettuce for ten minutes and cleaning the tadpole nursery, I pleaded with my boys to let the tadpoles go.

Their back legs had started to emerge. They had grown bigger. The space would be less, I pleaded. They looked plaintive and sad, and my elder son said the fish might consume them. We waited.

Then one day there was a typhoon prediction. I told them that the tadpole home could be blown down by the wind, and then they would be dead. I convinced them that the stream was a safer place for them. Finally, we let them go. Surya wanted to find them the next day. But luck was on my side and the tadpoles were nowhere in sight.

Now, whenever the frogs set up a chorus at night, my husband says that they are serenading me for feeding them well during their childhood! And as the grand finale, Surya did have a pet frog in our fish pond.

We even had a pet snail for a couple of days. All these events are things which, for big city dwellers like us, are unusual. We are used to seeing animals in zoos—well-regulated environments within jungles of concrete and cement. So nature residing within a two-tier city was a novelty for us. I bought Surya a book called *Snails,* in which they described how to make a snailarium. So of course we had to make one. When it started pouring heavily, we put some grass, leaves, and mud into the old tadpole nursery and put a huge snail in it. We let it go when it dried up after convincing Surya that it was not getting enough air to breathe in the little tank. It wasn't such a terrifying experience for me this time! For that season, whenever Surya saw a snail in our patio, he wondered if it was his pet or related to him. He compared the size, colour, and features of the snail with the one we had adopted for a couple of days. My ayis look on all our activities with a compassionate eye because they grew up so close to nature that they cannot understand our absolute fascination for these things.

The funniest experience we have had is of a pet egg. Aditya was twelve. Aditya's best friend, Antonio, wanted to grow a chicken from an egg. Aditya was doing this in class, but Antonio, a newly arrived Italian, being in a group that catered to beginners in English, did not get this exposure to science. In Suzhou, your best friend could be someone from a totally different linguistic and cultural background. In some places, such as Singapore, there are international schools that cater to needs of individual communities: American, European, German, French, Indian, Australian, and British. In Suzhou, there are only two major international schools that see you through from start to finish. Foreigners like us send our children to one of the two schools. As a result, we all learn that under the different garbs of culture and language, we have the same concerns and the same needs. Therefore, to make up for the deficit in scientific learning, Antonio took an egg from his mother's refrigerator, put it in a paper cup, drew a beautiful face on it, wrapped it warmly with a paper serviette, and put it near the room heater to incubate. He even took it to school in the pet lamb tradition of Mary. He was scared that someone, perhaps even his younger brother, would harm it if it were parted from him. So obviously, when he came to visit his best friend, Aditya, he brought it to our house. That day he didn't greet me in his usual pattern but rushed up the stairs with something concealed in his hands. Then the boys rushed out to cycle. I went up to Aditya's room and found the pet egg sitting under the blue neon light on

Aditya's desk. The lamp was on in bright sunlight. So I promptly put off the lamp. After some time, the boys came in. My husband went up to check on them. He found the lamp on and turned it off. Eventually, we were informed by the boys that they were keeping the egg under the blue light to keep it warm. Then Antonio's father, who was having a cup of coffee with us when he came to pick up his son, commented that they would eat up the chicken when it hatched. I have never ever seen a boy look sadder than Antonio at this remark!

The pet egg saga finally ended when Antonio's six-year-old brother broke the egg at school. In epitaph, Aditya told me the chicken probably had started developing, as most of the stuff inside the egg was yellow!

Luckily for me, currently most of Surya's friends have fish or nothing, or I might have had to keep an elephant in my garage!

CHAPTER 2

Holidays in China

My family loves to travel during school holidays. When we moved to China, we decided we would see as much of China as possible. The first place we visited was Hangzhou.

We went on the first of May, the first day of the famed May Day holidays. It was so crowded that the car moved at two kilometres an hour. It might have been quicker to walk. The human population and vehicle population were overwhelming. The lakes and the mountains that were the legendary beauty spots were covered with human population like a cookie on the ground would be with ants. The view was lost on us and to us.

May 1, October 1, and the Chinese New Year are holidays when all of China is out celebrating, a time when crowds conquer the tourist spots.

The first time we went to Beijing, it was around the October holidays. We thought, being Indians, we would not fear the crowds. And then, surprise, surprise! It was worse than Hangzhou. We were sandwiched in a crowd and had to move like the stuffing between two pieces of bread with the flow of the crowds. We were visiting the summer palace on October 1, and all we got to see in it were the swarming mills of heads around us. This time, we went to Beijing on October 1 with my mother-in-law because that was the only time my sons and husband could get away from school and work. We went on the train on October 1. That was not too bad, as we could evade the crowds in the superfast five-hour train journey. On the second, we went to Mutianyu again, a distant gate to the Great Wall. It was crowded but still doable. On the third, we gave a car tour to my mother-in-law of Forbidden City and Tiananmen. We did not get out of the car because all we could see was a colourful stream of people milling around the tourist spots like water in a pond! This time, because we anticipated this, we were wise enough not to get out of the car and explore near any of the sought-after sights.

However, we did get to see the famed Olympic Bird's Nest and Water Cube at close range at 9 a.m. These were not overcrowded then, but the crowds were building up while we were on our way out, and they had built up already when we got to Tiananmen Square and the Forbidden City!

December holidays are a good time to travel in China. The weather is pleasant, and people are working, as they do not have Christmas holidays here, or even a one-day holiday on Christmas.

We visited Xi'an and Guilin in December and had wonderful experiences. Both these places have fabulous and unusual mountains.

Xi'an, of the terracotta warrior fame, has the fabulous Li Shan mountains from which were made the mud soldiers to guard the tomb of the legendary Yellow Emperor. There is even a famous Hollywood movie, *The Mummy: Tomb of the Dragon Emperor*, which is based on a mythical, evil terracotta king. Of course, the real terracotta warriors were made for a king who was both cruel and self-made. He was the famous first emperor of China, Shi Huang Di, who lived more than 2200 years ago, around the same time that Asoka of the Mauryas ruled in India, my country of origin.

Films have been made about both Qin Shi Huang Di and Asoka. They both began their careers as great warriors and emperors. Asoka inherited his father and grandfather's kingdom. Shi Huang Di had to create his own empire by conquering six kingdoms. Asoka left behind messages of peace, Buddhist stupas, and an unstable empire that lasted for about half a century. Shi

Huang Di left behind the fabulous terracotta warriors to protect him in death and an unstable empire that did not last even another decade.

By the time he died, Shi Huang Di was one of the most feared and secretive persons in China. His second son, who took over, was misguided enough by his advisers to ape his father and outdo him in cruelty. As a result he was overthrown, and his father's grave was raided and set afire. There are legends about how his workers, concubines, and birds were buried with the king to serve him in the afterlife. The whole grave, which was like a miniature palace, has not been excavated fully for fear of ruining the legendary statues.

One of the first things we explored when we came to China was these warriors. For that, we made a trip to Xi'an, which in my estimation is one of the friendliest and nicest cities in China, with ancient history dating back six thousand years. Other than Shi Huang Di's mud army, one of the most ancient and fascinating finds is found in the Banpo museum, which housed the skeletons and remains of a six-thousand-year-old civilization found in China. This Neolithic civilization was largely matriarchal. They had strange marriage customs, which included no concept of commitment. A boy walked into the girl's home and woke up the next morning and went back to a normal life at his mother's in the daytime. A girl could have as many partners as she wanted, and a child born of her knew only his or her mother but not the father. It seems this kind of marriage still exists in the Yunnan province of China.

The other interesting thing that we saw in Xi'an was the Huaqing Springs Palace. Its history dates from the Zhou dynasty (eleventh century BCE to 711 BCE), when the Yellow Emperor built a palace here. Of course, additions were made by the first emperor in his lifetime, but nothing that one would notice compared to the terracotta men. Then various members added embellishments. What we see today was built by the Tang dynasty emperor Xuanzong for his concubine Yang Gufei in the seventh century CE. Yang Gufei is listed as the one of the four most beautiful women in China. What I found strange was that people revere her almost like a goddess. If you go into her history, you learn that it's murky and sordid. It seems she was married to Xuanzong's son to start with. The emperor saw her and fell in love with her. She was sent to a nunnery for five years and then reinstated as the emperor's concubine! It seems the emperor composed poems set to music and she danced to the compositions. Wow! How acceptable is that to you?

However, the emperor not only built a fabulous palace at the foot of Mount Lishan for his beloved, but also had a series of pools of different shapes there filled with water from the hot springs of Huaqing. This palace also housed Cixi, the last empress of China, at the turn of the twentieth century, and then later, in 1936, Chiang Kai-Shek hid here on his way out of China. On the glass panels of the windows that housed his rooms and office are bullet holes left by the Japanese soldiers as the Kuomintang leader escaped from the palace to the hills and then to Taiwan. From a distance, these ancient hills appear pyramid like, with green grass growing on them. The shape makes the hills look smooth and manmade from far. Closer, of course, there are uneven rocks, and the ascent is quite steep.

A fabulous guide took us around the Banpo civilization, Huaqing palace, and the terracotta warriors. She spoke in English and made the history come alive for us. She was fabulous in every respect except her choice of food. She insisted we savour local cuisine the day we went to Huaqing Springs, an experience I would prefer not to repeat. The food was oily beyond imagination. One thing I know for certain is that experimenting with cuisines is risky in China. Once, when we were new to China, we went to a Sichuanese restaurant in Suzhou, mistaking it for a Schezwan (Cantonese) restaurant, and the next day I was swollen with urticaria and had to take a ten-minute intravenous injection to come back to my normal state.

However, there was no such risk with the local food in Xi'an, as I could not eat anything much! My boys practically lunched on ice cream. The first day, we went to a restaurant near the warriors. It was what they refer to as an international buffet and not so bad. What was interesting in that area were the tourist souvenirs. We got some lovely hand-painted peacock tea cups. The next day our guide took us terracotta warrior shopping.

They have a separate outlet for making the warriors. The mud used by them is from Mount Lishan, the same that was used to create the Qin emperor's statues more than two thousand years ago. The two-thousand-year-old techniques are still used to recreate the warriors in that factory. My younger son was excited at this outlet. He posed with the warriors and statues. My husband thought it would be fabulous to have some life-size statues. Then I reminded him of our mobile lives, and he was forced to settle for a smaller set of five, with the emperor and his four ranks of warriors, which was more suited to our short-term housing lifestyle. The distinctive thing about these statues is that no two of them are identical. It seems the statues are modelled on the real soldiers in the army.

When we went to the museums, we discovered that we could not go close to the statues. We had to watch from a balcony; the statues stood in a kind of pit. But we had a totally enjoyable experience. There were a number of pits, each exhibiting different types of soldiers and formations. We could not go close to them, as Bill Clinton had, when he visited as the president of the United States, or Pablo Wendel, a German performance artist. It seems that Pablo Wendel was so fascinated by the soldiers that he dressed up as one of them in 2006 and stood in a gap in the line of the ancient warriors. He blended in so well with these terracotta gentlemen that it was a short while before the present-day living soldiers walked up to him and asked him to leave. But as Wendel was a statue during his performance, he refused to respond. Then six of the present-day soldiers carried him out on their shoulders. Eventually his clothes were confiscated, and he was sent packing in borrowed clothes!

Strange, isn't it—wanting to be a terracotta warrior? But to plan and have the courage to execute what he really wanted is what makes Wendel's story interesting. I wonder how many of us have the guts to do what we really want. Did the first emperor have the guts to do what he really wanted deep within his heart? Did his contemporary

Asoka have guts to stick to his convictions and materialize his dreams?

That is something I always try to get my sons to do. I even try to bake cakes on their birthdays to fulfil their bizarre visions. I have baked cakes and decorated them to make them look like a sun, a volcano, a chemistry kit, or an electronic circuit. Hopefully, if they see their dreams brought to completion, they will do what it takes to materialize their own dreams as they grow up. One of my happiest memories is when five-year-old Surya saw the sun cake I baked on his birthday and said, "Mamma! That is exactly what I wanted." I would do anything to see that look of wonder and joy on my son's face.

Talking of dreams and mountains, the other place that had dreamy mountains right out of a Chinese painting is Guilin, in the southern part of China. To add to its attractions, there is a 600,000-year-old cave with stalactites and stalagmites. It was the first time I saw a cave and stalactites and stalagmites in real life rather than in a geography book.

On the way to the hotel, we saw some unusual rock formations, like a U turned upside down, and sometimes in strange shapes. It was like structures out of a misty Chinese painting. We almost expected to see calligraphy on the edge of the scenery to complete the effect. These, we were told, were ancient rock formations that had inspired Chinese painters for centuries.

Guilin is a city with a total population of 620,000, and most of the town, we were told by our guide, caters to the tourist industry. The flavour here is essentially Chinese. In fact, when we checked the Internet, the only hotel we were familiar with in Guilin was Sheraton. All the others were Chinese.

Since the three men in my life need a hearty Western or Indian breakfast, we didn't take any risks. Sheraton it was! Our room had a marvellous view of the Li River, and the rock formations around it were intriguing. Aditya and my husband spent considerable time photographing the scene from our hotel window. We went out in the evening, returned to the hotel, and had our dinner. There was nothing we fancied eating outside. Most of the restaurants looked threatening. There was a pizzeria, but it looked like the kind of place where you could go green in the face. However, the street outside was interesting. It had different kinds of live music being played on street corners, a tae kwon do demonstration by children, and many tiny stalls selling local stuff, from silk scarves to handicrafts to fridge magnets. Within walking distance we found a water system called the two rivers and four lakes, which had fabulous lights. There was a boat ride on it, but the wails of five-year-old Surya prevented us from stepping into a boat.

The next morning, it was beautiful and sunny. When we looked out of our hotel room, we could see swimmers in the Li River. The temperature outside was about 11 degrees Celsius! I had heard from some of my Finnish and Swedish friends that people dug holes in the ice and went swimming, and I remember watching something to that effect on TV, too. But to see people actually plunge and swim in the cold river water made me feel shivery!

We started sightseeing with a visit to the ancient Reed Flute Cave. The caves were fabulous, but the lighting inside was a trifle garish. The stalactites and stalagmites formed a variety of pillars. There were structures like tall towers and pagodas. You could see things like cloud formations and whole townships in the palace nature built. It was strange to think that this had been used as a bomb shelter during World War II. In some places, the water was still dripping. Maybe a few centuries down the line, where the water droplets fall, there will be another new pillar. They had a light and sound show with lasers and sprays of water in what I would call the "womb" of the main cave. But nothing to beat nature!

Outside there were vendors selling bowls made from the rocks that are found lying in the caves. I bought a couple of them and also a Chinese male angel made out of wood. We had to bargain the prices down, of course. In retrospect, I really hope the bowl is as authentic as the vendors made it out to be.

Then we went to the 3.5-million-year-old Elephant Rock. This is a rock with an elephantlike shape on the banks of the Li River. There was a winery at the entrance, where they made the local rice wine. The smell was overpowering, and it took a lot of convincing to make the guide believe that we do not consume liquor. He was disappointed that we did not visit the winery, and we were relieved. There was a photo-shoot area where you could dress up in local gear and take photographs. Of course, my sons ran away from it while I stood and watched a pretty Chinese girl in a bright pink costume posing like a dancer for the camera.

There were men riding on tyres in the river and fishing. Later we realized that they were just posing for tourists! There was an ancient temple there and a Ming dynasty pagoda. At the temple were guardian stone lions. Surya decided to roar louder than these silent lions and drummed up quite a racket!

After the roaring and the jumping over rocks, my sons were hungry. The guide wanted us to try local food, and we insisted on KFC after our earlier experiences with different cuisines in China. I also had noticed that Guilin delicacies included silkworm noodles, horse meat, and grass snakes dipped in wine. Evidently men drank the wine to enhance their masculinity. I guess women kept off the snake booze! The guide and driver dropped us and went off for a bowl of rice noodles, which was fine by us.

Then we went for a ride among the mountains on a ropeway to get a bird's eye view of the limestone formations that dot all of Guilin and give the city a flavour of ancient Chinese paintings. It was an exhilarating experience, except that I was a little scared, too. Down below was a long path for trekkers. As we rode up to the mountaintop, other people rode down, and one of them decided to hawk and spit! It was a strange sight to see the man's spit suspended in the air. I was wondering if the spit landed on a trekker's head, what would the trekker take it for? Bird stuff, plant drool, or human hawk—yuck!

The view from the top was splendid, and as usual there were temples and, unusually, lists of some kind of Chinese genealogy.

We saw and experienced as much of Guilin as we could in a day. There is also the Li River cruise that one should not miss, but Surya was set against slow boat rides, and we did not fancy a ride with a whining five-year-old, setting the tone of our trip!

CHAPTER 3

Rides

THE RIDES MY HUSBAND and sons enjoy are ones that take away from my sense of relaxation. Early in our marriage, I realized I had married a man who loves amusement park rides that I do not like. My sons have inherited his fascination for these rides. The most nightmarish ride I had was in the Universal Studios in Singapore. It was an Egyptian mummy ride. I am proud to say I came out of it unscathed . . . because I was clever enough to shut my eyes the entire duration of the ride!

I like riding a horse, a camel, an elephant (which my husband refuses to try, pleading discomfort, but I say it may be fear), and even a pillion on a motorcycle (driven mostly by my husband when we were in the start of our life together). I rode an elephant and a camel in Jaipur with Surya. The elephant was much like the elephants I had ridden earlier in Assam and Singapore. But the camel was almost like a roller-coaster ride. When the camel gets up, you move down toward its neck, and when it moves up, you fall back almost to its tail. And when it runs, you feel you might be near the end of your existence in this mortal world. But there I was at the end, getting off with a brave grin on my face. I did not shout or scream at all because seven-year-old Surya sat with me. It felt good later. I always feel animal rides are a more unusual experience than mechanical rides.

When, it comes to rides in amusement parks, I normally prefer the choo-choo train rides. However, Aditya and Surya seem to have inherited their father's liking for weird rides. Wherever we go, we seem to be taking rides. I don't mind a closed cable car ride. I quite enjoyed the one that took us to Lantau Island in Hong Kong, where we saw a statue of Buddha the size of a mountain. The glimpse of this Buddha from the cable car was breathtaking—isolated, quiet, calm, and cool. The ride itself lasted for more than half an hour. We saw tiny boats on the sea, cranes lifting heavy things, and the endless water shimmering in the golden sun. The journey to and from Lantau Island was really an experience I would want to relive.

However, some of the rides I had the day before in Hong Kong Disneyland were not exactly my cup of tea. I volunteered to sit them out. The three men in my life absolutely insisted I accompany them on all the rides, as they do all the time.

The worst was riding through Space Mountain. It was pitch-black when the ride started. Aditya was with me, and Surya with my husband. I could see nothing, and then suddenly I was pitched into darkness and tossed like a rag doll on my seat. There was a whooshing sound and strange meteoric lights. The blackness was almost opaque. You could not see or hear a thing. We fell from a height and then we climbed to God knows where. All the time, I was terrified. My stomach churned into my head. I kept thinking if one of us fell down, we would be smashed. I was worried about six-year-old Surya. I started praying and weeping. When the ride seemed to slow down a little, I called out to my husband to check that Surya was all right, and he said that the little one was really enjoying himself! When we got down safely, Aditya was laughing at me. He recounted my reactions to his father. I was just very, very relieved to be on firm ground again. My husband said such rides are good for me as they take me away from my daily concerns. I know he is referring to what we call *catharsis* in ancient Greek tragedies.

The most cathartic ride I had was in Singapore. We rode on a toboggan in the pleasure resort of Sentosa. It was anything but a pleasure to me. I wanted Aditya to accompany me, but I was forced to go totally on my own because he was considered too old to have to be accompanied by an adult. What they did not think of was that an adult might need more support on a ride like this than a child! And I had to drive and steer with other riders whizzing past. My baby was with my husband. When I caught a glimpse of Aditya whizzing past on his gizmo, I tried to ask him to go slower; he's a rash driver. He should have let me go with him, but he just zoomed past. At a point, I was totally on my own with not a soul around me. I was scared of falling or crashing. When I stepped on the firm ground, out of what they called a *luge*, I was relieved. But within fifteen minutes, we started on a chair ride up the mountain, again Aditya and me, and my husband and Surya. I did not enjoy this ride, either, as there was no foot rest. I was scared my slippers, which were flip-flops with heels, would fall off my feet and hit someone on the head. Then I was worried that I would have to walk barefoot to our car.

Another terrifying experience for me had been a helicopter ride in Maui, Hawaii, when Aditya was six and Surya was still unborn. Aditya was not allowed on the ride. I sat squeezed between the fat pilot and my husband; I wore a vague smile since it was an office event and was being filmed. The three Americans behind seemed to be enjoying it. So was my husband. The view, I admit, was fabulous. But the helicopter was noisy and rickety. I felt exposed because the windows were huge and open, and we were flying quite high. If our seat belt malfunctioned and the helicopter took a spin exactly at that point, we all could have fallen out of the helicopter. Of course, it would have been a good time to use a parachute and try the safety gear on our backs, but I'm not sure I would have come out of it alive and unscathed. The pilot tried to put me at my ease by being jolly and chatty. But I could be at my ease only when the ride ended. I knew then, as I know now, I am not meant to be a parachute jumper.

The other ride, which even my mother professed to enjoy, is the maglev ride in Shanghai. This is a magnetic train that covers 40 kilometres in fifteen minutes. It's a shuttle to and from the airport from a certain point in the city. It peaks between 400 and 421 kilometres an hour for eight minutes. My husband says that there is nothing else like it. And that is a fact because this is the first commercial train of its kind in the world. Technologically, no one admires it more than me. But I always wonder what will happen if it comes to a sudden halt or the magnet does not function properly? I am always relieved when the fifteen minutes come to an end uneventfully. Of course, there is always the horrible turn where the maglev keels on its side almost as if it's falling off its track. And if I have lunch before the ride, which I do have every time, I feel the food lurch from my stomach to my brain.

The rides which all four of us enjoy are speedboat rides. You can feel the water spraying all around you and feel the sun and wind on your hair and face. We go for speedboat rides sometimes in Suzhou on the lakes that abound in this town. I feel these are similar to the motorcycle rides that I had in plenty before we got married. My future husband took me for many enjoyable bike rides.

There are also amusement park rides that are not as bad. I went for a log cabin ride on a water-based roller coaster in the Great Mall of America, and Captain Nemo's submarine ride in Disneyland, Los Angeles. These were before kids, and not so bad—in fact, quite enjoyable, too. One time in Disneyland, Hong Kong, we rode boats and rafts through Tarzan's make-believe jungle. There was a ride in a tunnel, not on a boat, but on a trolley, where I scored the highest by shooting the maximum number of *Toy Story* Zurgs while moving. My family says it was a fluke, but I say their grapes are sour because Mamma won.

The most extraordinary, extravagant ride that we took was the one to Beijing . . . on a high-speed train. We repeated this ride with my visiting mother-in-law because we were so impressed with it! This is a ride which all of us enjoy. The train moves at an average speed of 290 to 300 kilometres an hour, and we reached Beijing within five hours. We covered a distance of 1379 kilometres in record time. The landscape is highly visible, and we could perceive the difference between north and central China. Being on the train was comfortable because we could walk or stand when we pleased, and there was so much more space than in a plane.

In Beijing, the rickshaw ride through the narrow, old-fashioned alleys called *hutong* was special and entertaining. The good thing was that these rickshaws were automated, so the rickshaw drivers were not burdened by our weight—especially mine. It was lovely sitting on a crimson velvet seat and driving through alleys flanked by houses that were a few hundred years old. The experience had a flavour of antiquity with the comforts of modern technology. Mind you, the rickshaw driver who had the crimson velvet seat was enterprising. He caught us outside the Temple of Heaven. We were near the boundary wall, some distance away from the gates. When we said there were four of us, and his rickshaw was too small to accommodate us, he called his friend on the mobile. He had caught us on one side of the crossing. When we crossed over the overpass and came down to ground-floor level, he was waiting for us with his friend, who had a covered box-like rickshaw. We were forced to surrender, including the cash: 20 RMB for about 400 metres.

The temple is the largest wooden structure surviving from the 1520s. It is impressive and intimidating, especially when you see the markings for leading the sacrifice to its ultimate end. It has the dragon and phoenix motif running through its carvings and paintings. There is something pagan and daring about the spirit of this temple.

However, it is not the only interesting thing within the compound. The park, with its cypress trees and lawns and birds, is lush. There are trees with whirls on their bark, reminiscent of Van Gogh's *Sad Cypress*. The whirls are only on the bark, though, unlike the cypress paintings. The trees were labelled "Old Trees" in Chinese, said both of my sons. On our way back, we chased a beautiful blue-grey bird, and Aditya captured it with his camera.

The other interesting thing in the park was music. Some people were singing karaoke in Chinese, and some played the erhu . . . all at the same time . . . and no one seemed irritated by the other sounds. On our way back, we even heard blaring Hindi movie songs, the kind I do not like. People were doing line dancing to that.

One has to say the rickshaw drivers were superb. They found us . . . again. This time they took us to Tiananmen through the *hutong* of Beijing. That cost us another 80 RMB. A normal taxi ride covering the same distance would be less than 30 RMB—probably closer to 20. We paid for the flavour and experience, I explained to my husband as he told me irritably that we could have taken three taxis for the price he paid. The men earned their pay with their enterprise and glib tongues. Some people, like my husband and sons, would have noticed open dustbins in the *hutong*. I only saw the antiquity and flavour.

The third time, at Tiananmen, I spent some time looking at the sculptures outside Mao's mausoleum. These sculptures depict the workers marching in the people's rebellion toward an ultimate victory. The expressions on their faces depict anger directed toward achieving their end. The statues are vibrant and make one think. It makes me wonder: Can a movement borne out of largely negative feelings give way to a positive thought process and a positive, holistic society?

Another sight always makes me feel I am watching history in movement in this area: the roofs of the Forbidden City, which preen over the walls of Tiananmen. We went to the Forbidden City the first time and heard all the stories and saw the remnant artefacts. But I was a bit disappointed. All the stories related to us by the guide seemed to reflect an opulent and hedonistic lifestyle without any greater movement. Normally opulent hedonism at least yields some beautiful art, music, or culture. But the life that was exposed to us within the Forbidden City seemed to be largely opulent and sensuous *only*. What was interesting was that the guide claimed that the Forbidden City was initially constructed in Nanjing and moved stone by stone to Beijing. I wonder how long this took!

CHAPTER 4

The Great Wall of China

To ME THE MOST fascinating thing about Beijing is the Great Wall. I have seen the Forbidden City, Summer Palace, and Tiananmen Square. But for me Beijing means journeying to the Great Wall. We have been to see this legend four times.

The most fantastic thing about the Great Wall is its continuity and endlessness. And that is what it denotes. Its spans 2000 years of construction and an endlesss sense of length. Estimates of its length are between 1500 and 5000 miles. The materials vary from mud to sturdy stone. It starts in Mongolia and stretches to the coastal town of Shanhaiguan on the Yellow Sea . . . that's nearly up to the Korean Bay. It is a story that encompasses endless eras and endless tears. Thousands of labourers were buried under the wall through the ages. It encompasses stories of cruelty and legends of achievement and of loyalty. It has been much written and fantasized about. It has been painted by numerous artists in different styles. They have made films on it, even Bollywood movies. And of course S. T. Coleridge's famed *Xanadu* refers to it.

Twice five miles of fertile ground

With walls and towers were girdled round.

So as you can imagine, when I was finally on the Great Wall the first time, it was the ultimate. I felt this crazy sense of exhilaration coupled with euphoria. I could imagine ancients, especially unwashed Mongols, giving out blood-curdling whoops, riding on their sturdy horses, with both the horses' and riders' manes flying wild—riding to invade the plenty in China. I could imagine a delicate, frightened princess hiding, sheltered, and cocooned by the hardy soldiers behind walled mansions, protected not just by the walls of their palaces, but by the Great Wall, which grew greater with the tears and blood of the common man, who laboured to give his land the ultimate protection from invaders. I had tears in my eyes and also felt a sense of achievement because this was something I had wanted to do from my teens, and we finally did it the first time when I was past forty. And whenever I'm in Beijing, I like to repeat the experience.

The Great Wall was built to protect and unite the people of different kingdoms from invaders: the Huns and Mongols and other aggressive tribes outside the bounds of the Chinese empire. One of Aditya's humanities teachers referred to it as "a wall to pen in the sheep". But I think it's bigger than that. The Wall has become an embodiment of the Chinese spirit of endurance and hardship through the ages. It is a ballad to the blood and tears of the common population. It also upholds certain Chinese values that are unique to the nation. It makes China into what it is today.

The Chinese protected the country that was the centre of their universe (Zhong guo) from invasion by different cultures and traditions. While the rest of the world intermingled, the Zhongguoren (the people of the centre of the world) remained apart. Unlike its neighbour India, China for a long time was untouched by world events. I don't know if that's good or bad. Some people may call the Chinese insular. But I think their seclusion built up their inner resilience in a way that has helped them survive through thick and thin. It is not that other nations do not survive or suffer. But staying for more than half a dozen years in China, makes me realize how different it is. Sometimes I see fleeting similarities to the typical Indian in the common man, but that's because they are human and children of two great nations with immense history. But while China was the untouched centre of the world, India was the hotpot of all cultures. To be an Indian is unique as to be a Chinese, because we have the blood of most of the races around the world in the veins of India. Isn't that something fantastic, too? It's like being the two opposing poles of a magnet.

For all of us, the Great Wall has been a profound experience every time we have been on it. We drive down from Beijing. There are six entry points to the Great Wall from Beijing alone. The most popular is Badaling, with the statue of Jiguang Qi, the Ming dynasty's major architect. This man visualized and created what most people know as the Great Wall. He was a soldier and a creative visionary. He worked for ten years on the Wall. Then he fell out with the emperor and died in ignominy. However, his vision was so ingenious that it was realized even after he died, and today we have his dream listed as one of the wonders of the world.

On our first visit, we went to the entry point at Mutianyu. We went up on a cable car to the foot of the Wall and then climbed the steps. Ha! We were there at last. When we got there we realized that though it was the end of September, it was warm and sunny. We wanted Surya, then four years old, to take off his sweatshirt and jacket. Since Surya was fond of that outfit, he set up a wail of protest cum indignation. It lasted till we crossed through the crowds and came across cannons on the wall. Surya's protest gave way to admiration of the cannons. There was peace at last.

My husband and Aditya photographed the Great Wall and the fabulous scenery around it. I gazed beyond, dreaming as much as I could, till Surya expressed a desire to relieve his bladder. I had seen a Chinese boy of about five using the gaps in the wall to relieve himself, but somehow, that seemed a bit incongruous. So we decided to descend at the next exit to the mountains below. On the way, Aditya informed us his needs were similar to his brother's. As we went down the steps and on the mountains, Aditya spotted a donkey. He was excited and kept shouting, "Mamma, *gadha, gadha . . . gaa-dhaa . . .* gadha." A *gadha* is a donkey in Bengali, our mother tongue. Surya was equally excited. He went close to the donkey and probably would have pulled its tail if we hadn't stopped him in time. My sons grew up in Singapore before we moved to China and were unfamiliar with donkeys except in the zoo. Both my boys were excited to see the donkey, which stood patiently on the hillside, gazed at infinity and grazed in the shadows of the Great Wall.

We returned to the Wall. Now it was time for hunger. The boys had a banana each. We bought them from a vendor on the wall, and they were really expensive. Then it was time to photograph the praying mantis sitting and chirruping on the parapets. There were not just a few, but many of them, sitting at various points. We got off the wall in a chair that descended on a suspended wire, while fearing tears from hunger pangs would come from my sons. We had spent a couple of hours walking on the Great Wall. It was a fantastic experience!

We lunched at a restaurant called the Schoolhouse. This, again, was a memorable experience. We sat on the terrace and gazed at the Great Wall while waiting for the food to arrive. Surya talked excitedly of the donkey. So I asked him, "Did you like the donkey more or the Great Wall more?" Promptly the answer came: "Donkey!" As we all started laughing, he edited his statement and said he liked both equally! Well, that's a four-year-old trying his hand at diplomacy.

Then I was overcome by a terrifying experience. I found a giant praying mantis perched on my lap! As I screamed for help, paralyzed with fear, Surya laughed with glee, while Aditya and my husband focused their cameras on my lap. My husband asked me to hold still, as he feared the praying mantis would fly from its perch. Finally, a waiter from the restaurant came to my rescue. Everyone thought it was funny. Well—everyone except me. I screamed. After all, none of them had a giant praying mantis sitting on their laps!

I achieved a sense of immense satisfaction from walking on the Great Wall. I wanted to go back to it again and again. Next time I wanted to go to a different part—maybe Simatai, the part of the wall that's supposed to be most picturesque. Or maybe, Shanhaiguan, where the man-made wall comes to a halt in view of God's inimitable creation—the ocean.

We did go back to the Great Wall a year and a half later, but not to any of the places I had thought of returning to earlier. This time we went to Juyong Pass. We surfed the Net and found that Simatai required good hiking skills. With Surya being six years old, a difficult hike was not a feasible proposition. And Shanhaiguan did not seem to have suitable hotels close by. We needed one where we would be assured of a good Western breakfast, a minimal requirement for the three men in my life. We could find only some Chinese hotels there. A bowl of rice porridge is not exactly the kind of breakfast my adventurers can survive on. So we went back to Beijing.

We started out for Badaling. The scenery was breathtaking after we left the town behind. It was a bit cold and foggy for April, but we all know of the global changes in weather patterns now. There was this fabulous winding river and hills, just like in Coleridge's poem. On the hills, we saw the Great Wall stretching proud and long. We liked it so much that our driver suggested he would take us there instead of Badaling.

This was Juyong Pass. It was fabulous, like out of a picture book. There was an uphill climb. We could not go very far because Surya felt cold. In the city, the temperature was about 13 degrees Celsius. And here the temperature had dropped to 7 degrees Celsius, and there was a cold wind blowing. Higher, it was 6 degrees Celsius. Again, we had no choice but to head back. But we did explore the lower reaches—the bridges; the tunnels; the offices, where the Chinese Army officials would sit and plan their strategy; and of course, the cannons. Surya made a lot of funny faces and poses on the wall. We also bought some souvenirs and T-shirts for the boys with a picture of the Great Wall and writing saying, I Climbed the Great Wall. After all, they had both climbed the wall twice at a very young age, and that is quite an accomplishment.

There were no eating places around. They had a coffee shop, but its unsanitary condition would have required major compromises that we were not willing to make. So we went back to town for a late lunch.

My first experience of the Great Wall was breathtaking. The next time, it was fabulous, but we could not stretch out our time as we did at Mutianyu, for we were unprepared for the temperature difference between the Great Wall and the city. But I am glad I went back, and thought that maybe later I would get to go and meet the ghostly Qi riding his steed in Badaling.

The third time, I did see the ghostly rider at Badaling. Qi on his steed appeared to be a short man. Except for the statue, this was my first experience of wanting to be off the Great Wall. Not only was it crowded and touristy, but most of the crowds were aggressive Chinese. They pushed and jostled. And there was a long white tunnel that led from the cable station to the Great Wall. There were cable cars at one end and the remade Great Wall at the other end. It reminded me of labour camps and concentration camps. It was cold, windy, and crowded in the tunnel. I spent more time queuing in it than on the Great Wall.

Badaling was a big disappointment. I was so claustrophobic in the crowds that I could not enjoy the walls stretching out beyond. I think this is one attraction in Beijing that is grossly overrated. Though I must say I loved our Mutianyu and Juyong Pass Great Wall experiences.

I see Badaling as an interlude in my romance with the Great Wall, which to me is the most fabulous thing in China. I hoped to go to other parts of the Wall to relive the splendour I experienced the first two times.

In fact, the fourth time, I went back to the Great Wall at Mutianyu with my mother-in-law—who, despite her bad knee and inability to walk much, climbed the Great Wall and looked like she had conquered all the Mongolian hordes. It was more crowded than four years before. It had more restaurants, and they were building a new access. But still, it held its charm intact. The husband of one of my friends said that there was something about the Great Wall that made it truly spectacular despite the crowds and the reconstructions.

Perhaps it is a thing of the spirit that sustained the centuries that went into making the Great Wall what it is today. Perhaps it is a matter of getting in touch with the feeling of antiquity and longevity lying beyond the scope of everyday human perception that makes us cherish this snakelike wall that curls and winds its way over a large part of China, unifying it with its silent presence.

CHAPTER 5

One World

ONE OF THE MOST enriching things about living in China is the wide exposure you get to people of different countries. China, which was so insular in the times of yore, has opened its doors wide to foreign talent from all over the world. Therefore, on any given day you interact with people from six or seven countries, sometimes even more. You forget they belong to another country. You see them only as human beings. You have all the Chinese on one side with their centuries-old insular culture trying to gauge the other side, long-nosed hairy foreigners who have strange customs and ways. Mind you, even if the Chinese are always aware that foreigners are non-Chinese, they are friendly toward us. They welcome all foreigners with open arms, even though it is said they do it because they know we will spend in their country and enrich them. But I see nothing wrong in that as long as I am not fleeced.

Because of this culturally diverse community, our children have friends from all over the world. Their parties are multicultural and wild . . . and sometimes a bit sad, too, if it's a farewell party for friends leaving, which happens often with families coming on two-year expat assignments.

If you are familiar with *Alice in Wonderland*, you know about the endless party given by the Mad Hatter. I had such an experience once, when my sons invited their Finnish and Italian friends to spend the day with them before they departed for their home countries permanently. It began at 9.30 a.m. I had six overexcited children in the age range of six to fourteen spending the day at my place. Five were boys, and one was an unfortunate sister.

I told them what I thought would begin the day in a most peaceful tone. I said they could start the day with candy and a movie. There was a minor skirmish over the choice of film. Everyone wanted to watch something different! Movie choices ranged from *Bugs Bunny* to *National Treasure 2*. Finally, I had the younger four, their ages ranging from six to ten, watch *Over the Hedge*, and the older ones watched *National Treasure 2*. Battle one ended peacefully, and the substantial amount of candy, which they were supposed to munch on for the rest of the day, disappeared in the next fifteen minutes! They all had drinks after that, ranging from water to juices to hot chocolate.

I took pictures of them while they watched the movie. Leonardo, who was eight, watched the movie from under our centre table. Frail Finn Maya, ten-year-old Kalegh's younger sister, sat perched on the sofa back. Kalegh and my own six-year-old Surya lay on the sofa handles. None of them sat on the sofa seats. It took me back to Aditya's childhood. He used to jump while watching his favourite shows on TV. And when we took him to watch his first movie in a hall in Singapore, *Harry Potter and the Sorcerer's Stone*, members of the audience urged Aditya to lower his volume because they could not hear the dialogue. It was nearly impossible for us to contain Aditya's vocal chords, so for a long time we abandoned theatre halls for VCDs and DVDs.

In Aditya's room, fourteen-year-old Antonio lay on the bed, and my thirteen-year-old son sat ramrod straight on a chair watching *National Treasure 2*.

I had managed to finish cooking lunch when I discovered that *Over the Hedge* was over. More demand for candy and drinks. No, I said; lunch soon. But please, please, please . . . I gave in. The whole problem was I knew these kids so well and was so fond of them, and I knew that I may never see them again; so I could not be my firm self. Of course, that meant I would be willing to dance the hornpipe the rest of the day. I wanted them to have the best day ever that day in my house and always to remember each other with happy thoughts. I think children sense these things.

The madness started as I lay out lunch. Maya ate raw vegetables, plain rice, and fruits (watermelon and mango). She said she did not eat meat—eight and vegan? Well, we move early these days. Her brother ate mainly sausages, a sprinkling of vegetables, and had to be persuaded to eat his rice with the aid of ketchup. None of them ate fish or meat. Leonardo, who after turning eight had decided he was going on eighty, ate mainly fish. He said it was the best in the world. It made me so happy! He said he loved the sandwiches, too. Antonio stuck to sandwiches, meat, rice, and vegetables. The worst thing was Aditya was begging for meat, but I did not want to give him any. The day before, he was suffering from indigestion for overdoing his protein intake. I wanted him to stick to fish and rice. But, well . . . I gave in again, as Aditya's happiness is often defined by his stomach and taste buds. I just hope the girl he marries loves cooking and eating as much as he does!

After food, as I was a bit short on candy, they attacked my stock of chewing gum and finished it.

Then it was close to 1.30 p.m., and we exchanged kids with our neighbour. Maya went off to play with her Finnish girlfriend, Anu. Ansi, Anu's six-year-old brother, joined our horde, to the delight of his friend and neighbour, Surya. I must mention Maya had spent the morning with a bunch of boys who considered girls unworthy of their attention. But I always notice the boys are happy to harass them.

So there was general rejoicing among the boys over this trade-off.

Then there was the battle of the Wii—a strange invention that gets even the dads hyperexcited. Though they battle it out with their six-year-olds, they are beaten often by the youngsters. I had to restrict each pair to two turns. Kalegh, who did not want to play Wii, played computer games.

I tried to distract them with a train track, but that was not very effective. Then there was a demand for a chocolate-chip cake, and Kalegh offered to help me! He said he was a good cook. So when I heard one of them wanted to see *Mr Bean*, I was happy to ask Aditya to put it on. Then I baked my cake in peace, with only an occasional disturbance, including offers of assistance from Kalegh and demands to taste the cake from others. Kalegh had his second cup of hot chocolate and cookies while waiting for the cake. Finally, at teatime we had the cake, popcorn, and biscuits. I had two of the moms with me by then, and things seemed to be a little more under control.

And then came the grand finale. Since it was raining outside, and the World Cup matches being hosted by South Africa didn't start until night here, my half a dozen bravehearts became indoor footballers. They practiced penalty kicks in my home corridor. I moved to a flat between my two houses. Starting with Surya and Ansi through to Antonio, everyone stood in a queue and kicked the ball into the goal, my guest room door. It was confirmed that my guest room door was sturdy. Also, I am fortunate that no one lived on the first level. Otherwise, I am sure my neighbours would certainly have asked us to evacuate the flat overnight.

When the noise level started peaking to shattering levels, the moms in my house marched their wards home. And then there were only three, who played inside for some time. When the rain stopped, they went out to play football. We had a comparatively quiet dinner for three, and the last goodbyes were said.

I felt I had achieved one of the most astounding feats of my life—hosting and "ending" the Mad Hatter's party.

At this party we had children from only three countries. There are times when we have parties with at least ten different nationalities present. And most of the time we are not even conscious of it. We see moms and kids. The colour, the language, and the food does not matter much. What matters are the human interactions. You see the moms have the same concerns, and children play together without fear of racial or religious disharmony. So why is it we need these narrow walls that keep piecing mankind into narrow slices and causing disharmony?

When man came into existence, he walked the earth free of all systems and boundaries. There were no religions, no rules, and no customs. There were no countries, no passports, and no visas. There were no creeds, no beliefs, and no languages. To my understanding, might was right.

Then there were farming communities. Rules started being formed. Who formed them? The people. Was it a democratic rule or an autocratic rule? Then at some undetermined date, world history started. Then religions, states, and complexities crept in with so-called early civilizations. Were the people any less happy or any less evolved in their way of thinking? Were they good or bad? Did they have higher or lower standards than us? Did they have any standards? Did they have morals? I believe that morals and social rules came about for the sake of peaceful existence and to give people peace of mind.

I have read that long ago the Mongols did not bathe. They probably defeated half the world by the sheer stench of their bodies and bloodthirsty ways. Imagine having to fight against an overpowering smell! Can you imagine going close to a man who stinks like an unwashed animal, wears animal furs, and has dirty, uncut fingernails, matted hair, stained yellow teeth, and bad breath? Well, people who fought the Mongols probably had to. Kublai Khan was a polished version of his ancestor. But think of the hordes of Genghis Khan! What were they like? When they let out a bloodthirsty roar and raced on fast wild horses against the washed and clean armies, how do you think a bathed soldier would react to the combined stench? Would he be able to think and do what he had been trained to do, or would he recoil? Was there a psychological backlash?

When Mark Twain's Connecticut Yankee travelled to King Arthur's court, back in time and history, he was appalled by their savageness, fascinated by their simplicity, chagrined by their boastfulness, and could trick them because of his knowledge of history. The Yankee was probably thinking of the inmates of Camelot in the same way that impassioned missionaries and conquistadors of the eighteenth and nineteenth century thought about the natives they conquered in the hope of converting them into "civilized" beings.

World history is a strange thing. Man walked across the isthmus that joined Asia and North America and somehow went across to the southern hemisphere. (We do not know exactly how, unless we believe in the theories put forth by alienologists.) He settled the land and tamed it to make it habitable. He lived in sync with nature and flourished. And now, when mankind seems to have reached a high degree of evolution, we are spending a large part of our time trying to draw non-existent borders between ourselves. We initially made rules to live in peace and harmony. Each group of people had a different set of rules and beliefs because they found nature had manifested itself in different ways. So the rules to live in harmony had to be different.

Take clothing as an example. In the hot tropics, people wore less and lighter clothing. In India, the indigenous Indian women wore *sarees* and the men wore *dhotis*. When the Muslim invaders came in the fourteenth century, they introduced trousers for men and women (churidars, harem pants, and salwars) and long jackets (achkans) because they came from the colder regions to the north of the Indian subcontinent. They regarded any other costume as uncivilized. Then came the British, who wore collars and ties, and the women wore hoops in the hot Indian summer. They never adapted to native wear. Who were more uncomfortable for what they wore? And who were forced to leave?

In the twenty-first century, while we are trying to level out cultural differences and have taken to dressing to suit the needs of the changing climes, why is it we are still highlighting our differences of colour and creed? What is it that we have learnt from our study of world history? Only our differences? When will we learn from the past—the ancient past, when mankind walked to explore the continents and knew of no political and economic barriers? Why restrict ourselves to political and economic regions and classes when we could live in a world moving to explore the universe and finding alternative biomes for the existence and expansion of mankind?

CHAPTER 6

Oranges and Buddhas

MY HUSBAND AND I, and of course also our children, are Indians. My husband and I left India in 1991. We go back almost every year for a holiday of at least two weeks. My children were born in Singapore and have grown up in Singapore and China, but are also exposed to India for two to three weeks in a year. What does that make them? My youngest son has spent the major part of his existence in China. Yet in no way can we call ourselves Chinese or followers of the Chinese culture. What has evolved in our family is our own culture, which has influences from India, China, Singapore, and the rest of the world, since we have friends from all over the world.

Something that goes a long way in bridging this cultural diversity is the fact that all our children go to international schools and have friends from all countries. The children see no colour or racial boundaries when they make friends. The best melting pot for cultural diversities is children's birthday parties . . . those of the younger children.

Surya and his friends start planning their next birthday parties as soon as one party ends. Sometimes, if the older children splurge during their birthdays, it does cause a lot of concern among parents. However, parties and outings among the children are the best way of overcoming cultural barriers. They realize they have so much in common—including mothers like Hitler for the teenagers!

Aditya wrote a beautiful piece in school in which he called himself a citizen of the world . . . and aren't we all?

Youngsters sometimes stumble upon truths that take us forever to fathom.

Aditya is ramrod straight, much like a police lieutenant—strict, unbending, always trying to be taller than he is. When he was four, Aditya asked me how soon he could be a father in the family. I told him much, much later and asked him why he wanted to be the father. He said, "Because he is the most powerful." Now he is addicted to math and robotics. He likes his freedom, but he says he does not need physical freedom as much as mental freedom. He does not have issues about going out, but he says he needs freedom of thought. Man is born free, but everywhere he is in chains. Aditya is a bit Rousseauvian.

His best friend, Antonio, who returned to Italy, needs freedom of movement more than anything else.

My younger son, Surya, is nine, cute, and cuddly. But like his brother, he likes his freedom. However, he does not believe in giving freedom or respite to any of us, especially his brother. On holidays, he always picks on his brother whenever he has free time. He treats his brother's friends like his own. It is a task for us to keep him away from them. His favourite dream was and is Aditya turns younger and he turns older. He uses words that are bigger than his size, and has his teachers on his fingertips with his excellent vocabulary and his "I miss you" cards. He has many friends. There is Adrian, Surya's best friend, a little dreamer who has big ideas and lots of heritage from back home in Germany. Another friend was Jonas. Surya liked this long-haired Finnish boy who has taught him rollerblading and floor hockey. Jonas wanted to marry at eighteen, as it is permitted in Finland, and to have ten children together so that he could form his own hockey and football teams!

There was Ansi from Finland, too. He was the only brother in a family of three sisters. His second sisters was in Aditya's class. However, they did not interact much. The youngest sister, who is just a year older than Ansi and Surya, liked to befriend Aditya. They were our neighbours when we moved to an apartment in between our houses. Aditya was terrified of her. One day she went to the cycle parking to help him put his bike in place, and to his horror she managed to dump all the bikes on the floor. Aditya had to pick up more than half a dozen bikes and put them in order!

Another friend of Surya's who adored Aditya was a little French boy called Pierre, who was a personality in himself. He was a self-sufficient young man and elder brother to a cute, doll-like baby sister. He loved candy and blowing candles on everyone's birthday cake, including his own. Pierre developed such a liking for Aditya on Surya's birthday that when his parents bumped into us in a restaurant, he and his sister abandoned his parents and sat with us. I think Pierre pulled Aditya's nose all the time, and his sister, Aditya's ears. Aditya used to run when they spotted him at school till he was out of their line of vision.

Surya had another Japanese American friend called Mark. He liked to talk big. He would say: "I can count up to four thousand." Much in the tradition of his American father, who informed us that his seven-year-old memorized countries' flags in his leisure time, Mark was confident and spent a large part of the day declaring himself to be the best in everything. But he was a nice kid who pretended to fall asleep when he was made the goalkeeper while playing football, because he declared he got bored!

The child who Surya regarded as a football wonder was Ansi. Surya saw the legendary Pele make a fabulous goal in the movie *Escape to Victory*, and he declared that Ansi could do the same!

There was the German Karl, who is pint-sized but has a voice that can shatter glass. And Abe from the Philippines can shout for joy almost as loud as Surya; and believe me, that is loud!

Aditya's friends are a lot older and more reserved with me. But there was also the Finn Kalegh, who was three years younger, adored Aditya, and has returned to his own country. Both my boys were fond of him, as we were in the same compound together for three years. They collected tadpoles, made igloos in the snow, and played so many things together. Once, when Aditya was about twelve, Kalegh came to our house declaring a battle against girls, wearing a cloth armour, and carrying a plastic sword. Surya ran out with his stick, and Aditya was forced to follow, though a trifle reluctantly. Kalegh waged a war against the girls headed by his sister, Maya. The girls all ran away, and the boys decided to beat their next natural enemy—babies—which meant Surya. Aditya was, of course, a force to be reckoned with for any army against Surya. We mothers went and intervened and ended the battle.

One of the menagerie who cannot be overlooked is Leonardo, Antonio's younger brother. At five, he declared Aditya was his friend, and Antonio was three-year-old Surya's friend. Eventually, he and Surya did become companions. The two of them in a car were a lethal combination with their hysteria and noise. Once, after Surya turned six, Leonardo was spending the evening in our house, and my house agent was coming over to attend to some chore. Leonardo asked me who my visitor was. When I replied "my agent", he decided she was a spy. I clarified "house agent", but he spent all the evening with Surya under a table watching the two of us through a pair of binoculars!

The other binding factor is play. The quest for the supernatural is an obsession with all eight- and nine-year-old boys. Surya and his friends also have a fascination for the supernatural. When Surya was three or four, he would drape a sheet on himself and pretend to be a ghost. Then he took to calling his hooded T-shirts *ghostes* T-shirts. I never quite figured out why. Then he read books on ghosts and zombies that I did not approve of, and learnt to read fluently by age seven when his friendship with Gabe found its full bloom.

Gabe's elder brother Isaac decided to make a movie on zombies. A nine-year-old fourth-grader, Isaac, had to make up the zombies to look like zombies. He made up Surya's face with a green marker, and Gabe with less makeup, as he was a zombie in the making. Think of the joys of motherhood when, while taking some time off from kids, mommies were discussing books and up popped Surya of the green zombie face, grinning and sure of Mamma's approval. Well, Mamma was amazed, horror-struck, and partly amused! Isaac assured us the marker could be cleaned off. Gabe merely had a few suture like marks in many colours. I think they ran out of the green marker ink . . . only they were not willing to admit that.

Green-faced zombie Surya was proud of his movie debut and went around with his coloured face. In the playground, he petted the frog caught by Isaac. Maybe the frog felt more empathetic toward Surya, as they had almost the same colouring. The frog, of course, was smaller and had a moister and rougher skin!

Then came the time to go home. We were walking back since our compound was just across the road. On the way back we met Aditya's friend's mother and brother. They spoke to us but could not stop laughing when Surya proudly proclaimed that his makeup was for a role in a zombie movie. The Chinese security guard at our compound gate came out of his guardroom to examine the green man and could not stop laughing. Surya was beginning to figure out that people were not scared or impressed but were amused. Then my home help could not stop laughing when we reached home! Surya started feeling a little shy.

The time came to wash the goo off his face, but he didn't want his makeup removed! He said they were going to continue filming the next day, and he didn't want his makeup taken off. With a lot of cajoling, I managed to get him into the bathtub and cleaned it all up with a lot of scrubbing.

The next attempt at dressing up as a zombie was carried out by Surya himself. He received a bunch of washable tattoos from a classmate toward the end of the school year. The gentleman covered one arm with at least ten different tattoos. He said that zombies have all kinds of funny skin markings, and that is what the tattoos were. Next morning he was forced to wipe them off by his unsympathetic parents before he went to school. Alas, zombie experts Gabe and Isaac, did not get to approve of the makeup. Such are the cruelties exhibited by the race of parents, especially mommies!

Zombieism was a new experience for me because Aditya stopped at pirates, monsters, and tigers. As a tiger, he did bring down the curtain rods in his room, and as a pirate he jumped on furniture.

So I'd had many experiences—except zombieism.

And now, of course, I have the advent of zombies.

Surya and Gabe had stretched their imagination to even create zombie storybooks in school, fully approved by the teachers and given good scores.

They talked of ghosts and zombies all the time till they frightened themselves. Once Isaac told Gabe a story about a mommy who turned into a werewolf at night, and that night his mommy found Gabe weeping copiously as he feared his mamma would turn into a werewolf at night!

Surya made a beautiful terracotta structure which, thank God, he said was not a zombie. It was an island monster.

So—are we back to monsters again?

Well, maybe not! On Surya's eighth birthday, a bunch of spies found a dead body, Henry said, with the hands sticking out from the hedges of the tennis court. Surya said he saw the body in detail; it had its eyeball sticking out and its intestines were in the place of its brains! How gross can one's imagination run?

The nicest thing about this menagerie is their innocence and freshness. I love having them over, though they generate noise of unlimited proportions, trouble within limited proportions, and mess. They have so much warmth and affection that it is fantastic to be near them.

These are all children who come into our lives, enliven it for a few years, and then, like all expats, move on. We are left to make friends with the next expat kids and families. We are expats too, but we have lived here longer than most others.

With some friends, we cherish special experiences. Antonio's mom and I were good friends. Once we made a trip with both the families to an orange orchard. The owner of the orchard was a friend of their driver from his village.

As we approached his village, we could see orange orchards dotting the hills of the island. It was so beautiful. On two sides of the narrow road was the huge Lake Taihu, lapping its waves as if impatient to lick the juice of the delicious oranges growing on the hills of its islands. We were two families, Indian and Italian, going to a traditional Chinese village to pick oranges from an orchard. With us was Leonardo's American best friend. How exotic can one get?

A hospitable, aged Chinese lady let us tour her house. She gave us some green tea that grows at the feet of the orange trees in her orchard. The kitchen was a small, dark room with little space for movement. It had a built-in circular stove and utensils fitted to the stove, as it seems that traditionally, the Chinese do not wash some of the cooking utensils. She even had oranges growing in the land attached to her house. It was a quaint experience for us, and the mistress of the house was friendly and hospitable. She looked fifty but was closer to one hundred.

As we sipped tea, our boys had already started attacking the oranges in the trees near the house. It was time for us to go to the real orchard. We carried huge baskets to fill. The five boys, aged thirteen to five, were practically fighting to get at the oranges. They climbed with and without ladders and filled the baskets with excitement and enthusiasm.

With our baskets filled, we set off. Some of the villagers carried our baskets back. We started exploring the countryside. It was open, green, and clean to start with. We collected resin from trees. The locals said that they made medical decoctions with the resin. The boys were running all over and making discoveries. They found some interesting black stuff, which turned out to be grease from the trucks that had started intruding into the village as part of the building team. I don't know what exactly they are developing in these parts. And it's such a pity, because if modern civilization finds its way into this quaint village, the charm will be washed away. As it is, we learnt from our guide, a large part of the younger generation has left to find work in neighbouring towns. Much of the village was empty as we walked in.

Perhaps what we call civilization and modernization is another way of life, and it is as intolerant of what was past as the traditionalists are of the present and future. Coming from a country of mainly villages, I feel what we call *development* is subjective. For us, what is a necessity may not be a necessity for them at all; it could even be an imposition.

Take the case of a separate bathroom, which is a must in my scheme of things. Such a thing did not exist in the traditional Chinese house that we saw. There is a toilet bowl with full flushing mechanism in the bedroom itself. In China, many public toilets are freed from the cumbersome concept of doors. It is a bit uncomfortable for non-adjusting foreigners like us, but locals think it is perfectly natural to chat as they relieve themselves in public toilets. In swimming pools' changing rooms, women stay au naturel while changing and chitchat with each other in this state. It is a different matter that people like me have taken to avoiding public changing rooms in China. For the Chinese, modesty is not a necessity, nor is it in some countries of Europe. Many people think of these things in terms of being liberal. However, I look at it as lack of privacy. It's just a matter of perception.

Our kind hostess thrust sacks full of oranges and potatoes on us free of charge. These oranges were seedless and like manna from heaven. I, who normally do not like oranges, could not stop eating them. We distributed them among all our neighbours, drivers, maids, and others. And yet we didn't run out of them. In a country like China, this is an unusual experience, as you need to pay for everything here. You first need to pay your bill at a traditional restaurant, and then they serve you food! "Pay first, consume later" is the motto of this largely affluent government.

Notions of affluence or richness are highly subjective, and are determined by a person's frame of mind—what we call *attitude*. You can call a glass half-empty or half-full. You could be an optimist who feels that the morning sunshine is God's plenty or a pessimist who sees the sun as a cause of cancer, UV radiation, headaches and heat. Affluence and poverty are defined largely by a person's state of mind and culture. So you could weigh your riches against gold or God's sunshine and then decide which makes you happier.

This lady of the orange orchard definitely thought of herself as affluent, so she was happy to share her wealth with foreigners. She is one of the most impressive, independent, and enlightened women I have come across in this world, though she speaks only a Chinese dialect and probably has had minimal schooling, if any, because she lived her childhood here before the Maoist revolution.

On the way back, our friends bought pumpkins and pomegranates, and we bought just pomegranates from people selling their farm produce at roadside stalls along the village. There was a beautiful sunset that we could see along Lake Taihu as we drove back from the village to the city of Suzhou. It was like molten gold with splashes of rich orange juice brightening its intensity.

This remains an experience we will truly never forget. Most impressive were the simplicity of the lady who owned the orchard and the endless stretch of oranges that dotted the hillside of the island villages. I had never seen so many orange trees together!

Another fabulous fruit we learnt to relish is peaches—huge, succulent, sweet, and round. Peaches from the neighbouring town of Wuxi are famous. We bought some the first time from a roadside vendor while returning home with my visiting parents. The peaches come in around the start of summer in late June, and the season ends sometime in September.

We bought the peaches on our way back home from seeing the Lingshan Buddha in Wuxi. The Buddha at Wuxi is more than eighty metres tall. It towers against the Maji mountains, casting its blessing over a historic thousand-year-old temple. Though the Buddha was built around 1996, it adds to the grandeur of the antique temple and its surroundings. The other thing worthy of viewing here is the bath ceremony performed on a baby Buddha. This is depicted with a display of waterworks, music, and a revolving statue of baby Buddha. This performance is truly awe-inspiring.

The other truly spectacular Buddha in China is the Leshan Buddha. Located about 200 kilometres from Chengdu, the capital of earthquake-prone Sichuan, this Buddha is famous as the world's largest. It takes almost two hours to trek up and down the length of this sitting giant. The statue is 71 metres high and was built by a benevolent sage around the time of the Tang dynasty, almost 1200 years ago. It took almost ninety years to complete. Its builder carved a gigantic Maitreya Buddha in the mountain to control the waters of the turbulent river, which used to overturn the boats with its force. The large quantity of rubble from carving the Buddha was thrown into the river to calm and divert the current. This made life easier for those who were dependent on the riverboats.

The climb down was vertiginous, crowded, and narrow; the climb back to the top took one's breath away, literally and figuratively. The view was, of course, fabulous when you dared to stop and look around. The stairs were steep, ancient, and narrow, with a not-very-high parapet. A fall would end in a quick journey to the heavenly Buddha's abode! But wow! The place was crowded. And what was amazing was most of the tourists were local. And some of them were very old, maybe even octogenarians.

There was only a kiosk of sorts for refreshments. So we were fortunate to have carried sandwiches from the hotel. The bathroom, visited by my two sons, left much to be desired in terms of cleanliness, they said. My sons are experts in visiting dirty bathrooms!

However, the trip was a stupendous experience for us. We had experienced so many giant Buddhas: Lingshen in Wuxi, China, the bronze one on Lantau Island in Hong Kong, and the huge ones in Bangkok. There was even a Buddha in Bangkok covered with gold leaves.

The Le Shan Buddha looks like it has been carved out of nature and by nature. Its ancient heritage and the caves and water streams that trickle here and there make it one of a kind. It makes you sense the omniscience and omnipresence of God in nature. This is an experience and a story which I will never forget. The ancient sage, with his benevolence for mankind and his faith mingled with technical skill, could well typify what we look for in a modern-day scientist. The feeling you get is one of an optimistic continuity, beyond borders, time, and religions.

Chengdu is an unusual town. It has faced major earthquake tremors, but its buildings and the town remained unfazed by the natural disaster. This is a tough town . . . a town that can rear up its head and stand on its own. For one, it is very Chinese. There are many tribes living there along with the Han people. It is a prosperous town, with lots of designer and branded stores and a highly developed local transport system. Very few foreigners were visible in and around Chengdu. Most of the guests in Kempinski, where we were staying, were actually prosperous Chinese businessmen or otherwise affluent Chinese. They did not bend over backward to please foreigners as they do in most other parts of China. Most of the restaurants outside big hotels were Chinese. Where we live in Suzhou, there are oodles of Western restaurants, especially Italian ones. Not that they are tempting. But you can see a lot of foreigners and shops catering to their needs.

Sichuanese food is actually quite tasty—spicy and hot. We tried it the first night at Kempinski. The hotel had a five-star rating and had many eating places. However, its cleanliness and services left much to be desired. Also, the bathroom in our room had no lock. And mind you, this was one of the best-rated hotels in Chengdu we were able to find on the Internet. The concierge, who was Chinese and had almost no command of English, did not know much about the tourist spots.

Well, we did! We had researched the Internet before planning a holiday in Chengdu.

So the first thing, we were off to see the pandas. They live in a reserve in the Panda Research Centre. They're cute and well looked after. We saw funny red pandas, which look almost like foxes. They stood up on their hind legs and posed for the camera. And there were huge, rotund black-and-white pandas, which spent most of their time eating and sleeping.

There was one panda that I like to call the Papa Panda. (Of course, I do not know if it was male or female.) Papa Panda had a huge stick of bamboo, which he peeled and ate. First he sat with the stick of bamboo and chewed. Then he lay down and chewed. He relished his stick of bamboo. The peeled green bark of the bamboo fell on his huge, round paunch as he continued with his endless task of chewing. His full focus was on eating, and it was amazing to watch him enjoy his food. Crowds gathered to watch him eat. Then there was another panda, sitting close to where Papa Panda relished his snack. This one I like to call Mama Panda. (Again, I do not know if it was a female.) Mama Panda waited for Papa to finish eating and looked thoroughly bored. Her body language was like that of Penelope waiting for Odysseus to return home—patient, long-suffering, and a trifle bored. She waited and waited . . . till she fell asleep! After some time, having finished the bamboo stick, Papa got up—all the bamboo from his paunch fell to the ground—turned his back on us, and went away. Mama was fast asleep. It was like a domestic scene re-enacted—mamas eternally waiting for their spouses to give them time!

Our next stopover was the Jinsha civilization museum. This civilization dates back 2500 to 3000 years. Here in the museum lies the holy bird in gold that has become symbolic of Chinese heritage. Gold and ivory relics from the ancient Shu dynasty and an extraordinary gold mask also sit within the museum. We even saw the digs they were retrieved from. Surya was so excited by the mask that he sketched both the spot on the dig where it lay and the mask in a little sketchpad he was carrying.

The next day dawned again quite bright and clear for Chengdu. Normally, the weather in Chengdu is hazy and rainy, the driver told our family's Chinese communicator Aditya. My son did a second-level translation for us.

Both my sons speak good Chinese, and I speak bad Chinese, which I picked up from my maid and driver. Most people who serve us find it easy to understand me because my Chinese is at their level. An expat wife of Chinese origin once told me my Chinese was low-class. I found this linguistic class distinction in an otherwise communist country fascinating. But then Henry Higgins could always identify people from their accents and said poor accents condemn people to the gutter. Well, poor Chinese certainly will not condemn me to the gutter. For me, language is a way of communicating effectively. Literature is a different issue. I am not much into Chinese literature. History gives out much of it was destroyed over the years. What is left does not fascinate me enough to learn the language.

It is much like exercise. People exercise physically to keep fit and healthy. Does it keep them happy?

I have another theory about keeping fit and healthy . . . .

CHAPTER 7

Sweating It Out

EXERCISING FORMS AN IMPORTANT part of expat preoccupations in China. Sweat pouring down their faces, dressed in tight exercising gear, my friends and neighbours exercise their way to health . . . and, incidentally, a good figure. Some jog even in the rain, some do belly dancing, some do Zumba, some culture yoga and Pilates, and a few swim—that's non-sweaty. Some go to the gym and use exercise equipment, and some go to the spa and massage to sweat and beat out their fat, respectively. Some say they feel healthy. Some say they feel beautiful. Some sprain their ankles and some break their bones. But they all believe in exercise . . . sweating it out.

Once a friend insisted I add to my breathing exercises by walking briskly with her. I merely do *Pranayama*, a kind of yogic breathing that helps me manage my body and mind and takes ten minutes at the most. She insisted I walk fast to keep more fit. We did it her way for a few days, and then it happened . . . we had to stop our jaunt completely because she developed a sprained ankle while doing Pilates! And the wretched ankle refused to heal properly despite physiotherapy and high-end Chinese medication. Pilates, said my good Italian friend, who was as passionate about exercising as me, is Hollywood's gymnastics.

Another friend, a Finn, told me Pilates is a gentle kind of yoga that does not force you to perform beyond your ability. This friend, who took me to the gym once, developed a cold after that, and luckily (for me), I could not continue my training. The only time I went with her, I told her I would go on the cycle and exercise on it up to the count of ten. She agreed. And then, when she started the contraption, she refused to close it for ten minutes. She said a count of ten was not long enough!

Getting back to the story of Pilates, I always think of Pontius Pilate of Judaea who ordered the crucifixion of Jesus Christ. I wondered if he had anything to do with this form of exercise. When I surfed the Net, to my surprise, there was no reference to Pontius when I keyed in "Pilate" but a reference to this form of exercise named after its founder, Joseph Pilates, in the 1920s. It seems he developed it for POWs of the First World War. Now, it is popular among all the fitness addicts of the world. I wonder if these people think of ancient Pilate when they do this form of exercise. I wonder if they have wounds that need rehabilitation, like the POWs.

Well, to write in exercise terminology, when I jogged my brains (not raced them, as racing was taking them nowhere at that point), I recalled that the World Wars popularized existential philosophy with a tilt toward nihilism. This must have been popular among the surviving POWs and their families and friends. That is why maybe, when you surf the Net for *Pilates*, you come across jubilant Joseph's name before Pontius's. Religion and history have been flattened by fat-free abs and the necessity to maintain them. Probably, as I do not have nor do I aspire to have flawless abs, I even have a fleeting regret toward the choices made by the majority of mankind. In the quest for flat abs, are we losing out on the wonders in the universe? Are we forgetting that we have come this far by putting mind over matter? Are we losing out on the fun of living in our fear of becoming unhealthy, old, or diseased?

Once, I became convinced that tightening my abs with massage could be a good thing. I had lost weight over years doing yogic breathing exercises. My stomach skin grew loose as I lost the fatty deposits underneath. I felt a bit uncomfortable. One of my thirty-something neighbours lost her tummy fat and looked toned after a month or two of Chinese slimming massage. I thought maybe I could tone myself with the same massage. So I asked her for the address, and equipped with a card, I went to the massage parlour. What I overlooked was that the card was entirely in Chinese, and I could not read the language or verify the name of the shop. The shop was inside a housing compound. I went into this very pink place, showed them the card, and asked them in my bad Mandarin if they were the massage place indicated on the card. They said yes, they did give slimming massages. I enrolled.

When I went for my first session, I was asked to talk to the boss, an extremely waxy, slim lady with long hair. If she dressed in white and floated, you could mistake her for a long lost Chinese spirit.

She brought out lotions and potions and tried to convince me that the stuff was good for me. She also wanted to inject me with some brown liquid and apply patches so that I could lose weight in two days.

I was adamant. I refused.

I want only massage; I insisted.

She agreed and told me I had to pay 3900 RMB. I paid.

I was handed over to a twenty-year-old masseur. To my surprise, she put cups all over me and used a lotion that was supposed to increase my metabolic rate. She also tried to convince me that the medication was good for me. I wanted my money back. Lotions and potions are not my scenario. These things are often banned outside China. My masseur told me she suffered immense pain from the injected medicine and slimming patches . . . as if it were a virtue.

She told me some amazing things. She said no one would love or marry her if she were not very slim! Breast-feeding is bad for the figure! Women need to be slim. Men could be fat and ugly!

I wondered which century she belonged to. Did women's emancipation never reach her? I am not talking of women's liberation as a bra-free existence, but of treating women— womanhood and motherhood—with dignity! The boss told me I should stop eating and drinking cold stuff to be as beautiful as her. Beautiful to her is synonymous with being ghostly thin! She never eats watermelons or ice cream, or drinks cold water. She told me beautiful women cannot eat half the things in the world, and have to eat very, very small quantities of food. They can bathe only twice a week. Other days they can soak their feet in hot water after eating dinner. She offered to give me a code of food and conduct to stay slim, and in her definition, beautiful!

After two sessions I was also told that the programme would last for ten days only! I was totally amazed. I was amazed that my friends had signed up for three months for 3100 RMB. I argued to no avail!

One day I decided to discuss this issue of the slimming massage with my neighbour. She heard the whole story, listened to my descriptions, and then said the whole thing sounded strange and differed vastly from her experience! It sounded like another shop, as she received only massages for half an hour without lotions and potions! I went back the next day and checked with the masseur if there was another massage shop in the same compound. She replied in the affirmative. The mystery was solved. I wanted my money back. They refused. They asked me to come back later. I upset a cup of tea on the table and threatened to upset the fish tank, too, if they did not return the leftover cash! They hastened to return my money. You may wonder, *Why such extreme measures? Are you mentally afflicted?* Getting money back from such small-time Chinese businesses is difficult.

Let me tell you what I had to do once to get money back from a Chinese landlord in Singapore.

My husband and I were young then. We had no children. We had just obtained our permanent resident status and were thinking of buying a flat. With that intent, we contacted a house agent and went to see some houses with her. When we expressed a little interest in one of them, the agent and the landlord insisted we pay a non-refundable deposit of S$5000. They practically coerced the cheque from my husband.

We went back home that night and realized that we did not at all want the house. The next morning, I called up the agent and told her we did not want the house. She told me the money was non-refundable. Then I started spinning my tale. I told her that I felt the presence of an evil spirit in that house, and the feng shui did not suit me as I felt sick after I got back. I also got bad news from home, I added. In Singapore spirits and ghosts are revered by a large part of the Taoist Buddhist population.

There was a long silence at the other end. At last, the agent, a Chinese Singaporean, said, "You should think before you pay. I will talk to the landlord. You contact him in fifteen minutes and try to get the money back before he cashes the cheque. Take down his number." I did not point out to her that she did not give us a chance. I called the landlord fifteen minutes later and repeated my story. He asked me to go to his house and pick up the non-refundable cheque immediately! Our non-refundable cheque was refunded!

Long ago, before I tried massage, walking, or the gym, I tried to lose weight by swimming. I learnt the breaststroke and swimming at the age of twenty-four in Singapore. I started exercising by swimming for a few months. But on the way back from the pool to my flat, there was a bakery that sold vanilla cream buns. As I would be ravenous after exercise, I had one every day. I really enjoyed the snack. At the end of a couple of months, I had not only become brown-haired and brown-skinned (as the pool water bleached my hair and the sun burnt my skin), but also had put on a few kilos. Then, because I had started teaching, I had to give up my romance with the pool.

Now, after two children, I float and try to discover new strokes while lying on my back in the water and paddling short distances with God knows what stroke. One day, as I floated in the pool and my sons swam, a neighbour informed me swimming healed her backache and got rid of her fat. Well, good for her. Then she suggested I try my footwork and handwork with a board like her. I baulked. I enjoy the water and have no intention of making it my mission to conquer it. The water in the pool enabled me to frolic with my younger son. This is one of the things I enjoy purposelessly. Unlike my neighbour and a whole bunch of good women, I like my ability to have fun. Another neighbour offered to spend time checking why I could not swim longer distances anymore. While I am grateful to these ladies for their concern over my layers of flab and their persistence in sticking to me through thick and not thin, I wish they would enjoy me as I am. I still feel sixteen. One neighbour said I behaved like twelve. Well, either way, I do not want to be in anybody else's boots. I still feel young and beautiful most of the time, I still feel enthusiastic over things. I can still laugh like a child and lose myself in the wonders of the universe. I still believe in happy endings and believe that there is a solution to every problem we encounter. I like people to be happy. I believe happiness leads to good health and well-being.

For me happiness comes from being with my family, cooking, eating what I cook, and jogging my mind and not my body. I think being overconcerned about one's weight and fat leaves people so unhappy and unconfident that they fall prey to different ailments.

Once a teacher in my son's school asked me how I stayed so cheerful most of the time and looked so young. I told her my formula: do exactly what you want and what you know to be right, and you will never grow old or be unhappy. Any amount of Pilates for flat abs and bodybuilding will not change this fact. I am so sure.

CHAPTER 8

Flying

HAPPINESS IS SUCH A subjective thing. For some it comes from running and feeling fit. For others it comes from emailing. For others it comes from writing. For others it comes from doing sums. For others it comes from seeing new places . . . though sometimes the process of travelling to the new place may not be enjoyable to all parties.

There was a time when I did get happiness from flying in planes to new places. It gave me a sense of freedom and the luxury of being free from the daily hum of life. But with two sons, over the years I have ceased to feel the same sense of exuberance. I still love to explore new places, but the plane journey, the before and after, are experiences that I feel only a miracle sees me through every time.

Aditya and Surya grew travel savvy at a young age. A few years ago, on our way back from Singapore to China, the boys—actually Aditya—discovered a drinking-water cooler in the aircraft. Aditya drank water from it thrice, five-year-old Surya five times, and their father, only once. Through the entire flight, with a few hundred people aboard, I never saw anyone else use it! Well, at least someone appreciated the airline's effort at making passengers self-sufficient. Of course, juices and water were offered a number of times by the air hostesses. While that was sufficient for the rest of the passengers, my trio felt the need for more hydration and saturated themselves at the aircraft's fountain. Surya also needed to go to the bathroom four times in a four-and-a-half-hour flight. And as soon as the plane landed, Aditya declared he had to go to the bathroom even before we deplaned, while we waited for the door to open.

Earlier, at the airport, Surya was delighted with the joys of drinking water from a fountain with due encouragement from his dad. He thought it was the greatest way to drink water. I personally find such practices undignified and messy. But my trio never tires of exploring every possible thing anywhere and everywhere. They make sure I never have a dull moment in my life.

Getting back to that memorable flight back from Singapore, I recall a young gentleman of about four or thereabouts who wore a helmet on his way to the flight, on the flight, and later. He was still wearing his headgear at the luggage belt after we landed. I wonder how comfortable his parents were with the situation, as he was in his headgear for more than five hours!

Another gentleman, aged no more than six months, entertained us with incessant protests in the form of wails. He was hungry. He didn't like being belted. He needed to crawl. His ears popped . . . etc., etc. These are, of course, my guesses based on his actions that I could observe from my seat as Surya slept on my lap. I used the toddler's wails to make sure Surya did not cry. I told him that only babies cry when their ears pop and gave him a candy to suck when he woke up complaining of ear popping. Not being a baby is something Surya is always willing to justify, as his elder brother and his friends always tend to call him one. At eight, Surya dreamt of being sixteen. At the age of five, Surya told me maybe he could be ten on his next birthday and taller than his brother. Around the same age he had also confided that when he grew older than his brother, he would . . . And promptly Aditya explained that even if some day he grew taller than him, he would never be older. Pretty much what I kept reiterating to Aditya, since he was already nearly a head taller than me! Surya has adjusted himself to the fact that he will always be younger than Aditya. Thank God for small mercies!

During this flight, Surya and Aditya had disagreements. Surya learnt he could imitate Houdini and wriggle out of his seat with the seat belt on—definitely not a skill to put his parents at ease! I even had to threaten the two boys with, "I will send you to two corners of the airplane if there is any more misbehaviour." How much more entertaining can a flight get? It's like living through a comic strip!

The worst experience I had while travelling was when Aditya threw up and developed a 102 degrees Fahrenheit fever in the airport on our way to a three-week holiday in India. We postponed our flight and travelled a week later with a healthy child. Of course, our holiday was shortened by one week. Aditya was two years old then. Aditya started flying when he was nine months old. He never appreciated being belted and always voiced his protests in a loud voice. He did not even approve of bassinets and such trials.

His younger brother took after Aditya in these matters and made sure in a loud voice that we all understood his likes and dislikes, which did not entertain any of the other passengers and added much to our embarrassment. Surya at least enjoys the on-flight meals. Aditya never liked anything except home-cooked food. So either Mamma would cook or his grandmother would make sandwiches. All things to make travel more convenient for us! Now, of course, he looks forward to all kinds of food—even plane food. So I don't need to pack meals for on flights anymore.

Post-infanthood and post-bassinet, Surya and Aditya have always looked forward to their plane journeys, and I always look back on them and wonder at the miracle of having come through another ordeal successfully. And there is, of course, my husband, who always complains of the quantity of luggage I carry. I have never been able to appreciate his concern, which is heightened by my father's inconsiderate jokes about the bags and baggage I travel with! I sympathise with the fact that my husband needs to lift the luggage off the belt and to and from the trolley. Perhaps that is why God gave us two sons—to help the father carry the burdens of the mother!

One of the things expats in China seem to revel in is travel. And so do we—within and without China, within and without our city. We just pick up our bags and go, sometimes by airplane, sometimes by car, and once in a while by train.

There are some favourite destinations wherever we go in almost every city, and one of them is zoo.

I live in a zoo, figuratively at least. I visit zoos around the world. I do not particularly like animals, but I still have been to a lot of zoos because my sons are almost like inmates of the zoo. Aditya, at the age of six, delighted tourists in the Singapore zoo by shouting that he was visiting his great-great- . . . -many-great-grandparents in front of the orang-utan cage. He told me they were his worthy ancestors and also mine. While at any point, scientifically, this cannot be disputed, I consider ourselves a trifle more advanced. Of course, my sons climb everything, ranging from furniture to grills to trees to rope walkways. They like to swing. Often their behaviour and that of their closest friends is like that of their ancient ancestors.

Surya at five even brought home a book on monkeys for reading. The then twelve-year-old Aditya, the one who loved orang-utans at six, smirked over his homework as I had to read out two closely written sheets of monkey facts with imaginative interpolation by my little darling.

My sons always think visiting a city is never complete without a visit to the zoo. In China, we have visited zoos in Suzhou, where we stay, two in Shanghai, and one in Nanjing. Zoos in Beijing and Xi'an were left out because after seeing the Great Wall, Terracotta Warriors, and other wonders, we didn't have any time to go to the zoos. Also, you feel sorry for the animals in the Suzhou and Shanghai zoos, as they are not only caged but kept in a crowded small area. I think most zoos would be disappointing after visiting the Singapore zoo.

While on vacation in Singapore, we always visit the bird park, the zoo in the daytime once, and at night again for night safari. The zoos are fabulous, with adequate facilities for both men and animals. It is an open-concept zoo, and the animal trainers actually seem fond of the animals.

We went for an elephant ride once. My husband, as usual, did not ride. He said he needed to take the pictures. But my sons and I had a fun, bumpy ride. Aditya says he felt ticklish because of the elephants' movements. But I say if you move in the right rhythm, it does not feel ticklish at all, and you feel on top of the world.

Another place where I had a good ride was in the Shanghai Animal Park, the more interesting of the two zoos, where we rode a camel. This was before I went for the camel ride in Jaipur. And then we went to visit the animals inside an open enclosure. You get to visit the animals in an air-conditioned bus as the animals roam around in their reconstructed natural habitat. Sometimes the bears or leopards like to chase the bus. My children love it. Surya gets almost hysterical at times

We have visited the Delhi zoo a number of times when we have gone there. In addition, there is the deer park. However, again these creatures are in cages and look miserable. In Dehradun, we have cows and monkeys galore in addition to a small park with animals in cages. I feel sorry for these caged animals. We have visited a couple of zoos in USA before we had kids. I even visited a zoo in Oslo, Norway, where I was taking a course in economic development studies.

I was twenty-something and went to the zoo with my friend and roommate, Jane. We were fascinated by some miniature horses called fjord horses. Jane wanted me to photograph her against the horse enclosure. As she posed and I photographed, we found her jacket was a source of masticating pleasure to one of these creatures. We had to free the jacket before proceeding further.

My husband and I toured most of the Minneapolis zoo by train, as it was frozen outside. It was interesting looking at the animals on snow. They were like moving miniatures from a distance. My husband got a better view with his telephoto lenses. But I remember the big, hairy, ugly spiders, which I did get to see at close quarters.

There was a zoo in Vallejo where I watched exciting whale shows and saw a tall giraffe eat leaves with a forked black tongue! You get to see plenty of giraffes in the Singapore zoo, too. But somehow they seem smaller than the ones at Vallejo.

But the zoos in Singapore still seem to be a hot favourite. Surya used to chase the peacocks there when he was small. Aditya spent a lot of energy drawing parallels with his and mankind's Darwinian ancestors. Once my sons were fascinated watching lions indulge in the daily clearance of their bowels after watching them eat. They like to converse with the monkeys and stare at the elephants. The two gentlemen have also tried their hands at feeding animals there. I have a picture of my fifteen-year-old and eight-year-old feeding giraffes. They had the same kind of expression when they posed with the giraffes: embarrassment for being photographed in front of so many people with the giraffes and pleasure and wonder at having the opportunity to do so.

We liked the animals at Nanjing, too. They had noisy seals that seemed to be conversing in delight across glass barriers. Aditya was especially delighted. And Surya was fascinated by the towering height of the polar bear, a couple of metres tall. The polar bear liked to be petted. I saw him reach out to a zoo employee inside his enclosure to get petted. Surya was also fascinated by a cement igloo inside the indoor zoo. He kept running around the igloo with a toy suitcase in his hands. Only the lure of the polar bear seemed to get him away from it. As usual, Aditya photographed things as long as his camera batteries functioned. Largely, whenever we depend on him to take a picture, Aditya's camera batteries malfunction. During the total solar eclipse in China in 2009, I had to resort to last-minute photography with my cell phone because Aditya informed me just as the eclipse started, "Mamma, I am out of battery." I believe this is a common malaise which afflicted both him and his friend, Antonio. Now we have bought a good camera for ourselves to avoid battery unreliability.

I personally think I have visited enough zoos for a lifetime, but I am sure my children think otherwise. I like looking at pictures of animals once in a while and ruminating over them from a distance, where there is no heat and there are no horrible smells or crowds. Maybe I prefer looking at fields of flowers without insects outdoors. As the worthy Wordsworth said, "For oft when upon a couch I lie in vacant or in pensive mood, they flash upon my inward eye which is a bliss of solitude . . . and then my heart with pleasure fills and dances with the daffodils."

Museums are another favourite with my sons.

We went to an automobile museum in China recently. It is located between Suzhou and Shanghai in a place called Anting. My boys—all three of them—just loved it. The museum is equipped with antique cars, modern eco-friendly cars, and cars through the ages. They even had cars with two engines and two steering wheels, though I could not imagine who would want to drive a vehicle like that. They had cars from Europe and the USA and even a few Japanese cars on display. I was most fascinated by the elegant antique cars. Most unattractive to me, but attractive to my men, was a car that hung suspended from the ceiling, exposing all its engine and gadgetry. The boys spent a long time with their dad watching it, as if it were a Van Gogh painting—which reminds me of the experience we had seeing the great artist's painting while vacationing in Singapore one year.

We went to an art exhibition with Van Gogh paintings projected all over the room. It felt like walking into the paintings. I was excited, as I had seen the originals at the Van Gogh Museum in Holland in my teens. My husband and kids were excited and fascinated, too. They had soft Western classical music playing in the background, and projections that brought the paintings to life and created a play of strokes and lights that I had never savoured before in an exhibition of Van Gogh's paintings.

There was another exhibition in the same place which my children just adored—the works of Salvador Dali.

There was a projection of Dali's face on a smoke curtain which Surya loved to run through, and there were his surreal sculptures and paintings that made them think and laugh. At the end they bought Salvador Dali moustaches and wore them every now and then! They loved the flamboyant look of the moustache, which resembled some of the whiskers we saw in Rajasthan, India.

CHAPTER 9

This Is China

IN CHINA THERE IS an absence of media as we know it in the rest of the world.

We do not get YouTube or Facebook directly. We do not get satellite TV, except illegally. You can get Facebook and YouTube, too—with the help of a virtual private network (VPN). Occasionally the VPN is difficult to access, too. Expats grow unhappy, especially when the VPN is blocked or jammed due to excess traffic.

But is it such a bad or difficult thing?

I lived avoiding Facebook till a school friend of mine based in London lured me into it with the temptation of accessing old classmates. And then began my woes. There are too many voices in Facebook. I would call it noise. It takes away from the harmony of our lives. I do not understand why I have to share everything with everyone on my social network. I discovered I do not want to know things about many people that they put on Facebook. I liked the mystery! Facebook, to me, is like a faceless monster trying to engulf our individuality.

YouTube, again in limited doses, is not bad, but too much of it takes away from human intelligence and existence. Watching an occasional movie is nice. But I would be worried if my kids were hooked on either YouTube or Facebook.

In China, of course, you have the parallel of YouTube: Youku. I don't know if they have anything like Chinese Facebook. The majority of the population of China remains even now untouched by the cultures and customs of the outside world. To maintain this pristine balance and have most of the people think in sync with them, the Chinese government implemented media monitoring. For the expats who have been exposed to so much of media, they have a little more leeway: the VPN.

Sometimes I wonder if all this exposure to media is good. In India I trained as a journalist, where we were taught a maxim: "Good news is no news." And that is what the Indian media still seems to believe. An Indian newspaper nowadays seems like a bunch of bad and sensational news put together. The Indian newspapers deal with things that sell. Lack of morals and values are always appealing, and aping those negative values is always easy. Kids find it easier to indulge in sensuality than to hold back. Moms talk of modern society where kids have to be given leeway to indulge in drugs, smoking, and sex.

Perhaps one of the strangest phenomena is the highly value-based Amish society in the USA, who ride carts and still do not use electricity. The women wear long dresses and caps and the men drive buggies. You have to have a special permit to even own a cash counter in a shop. I wonder how many people from India visit the Amish when they go to the USA? They think westernization means negative family values, drugs, and parties. I am not talking of living like the Amish, but of holding on to what is positive in our culture—family and family values, with the mother as the person who holds the household together.

Nowadays, mothers and fathers both contribute to the household income, and if they are affluent enough, a maid looks after the kids and home. So effectively, affluent Indians live in a maid's house and the kids are brought up by maids.

In China, when both parents earn their daily bread, the grandparents take care of the children. In an American or European home, even though a mother works, she looks after the kids and home with some childcare support. A small percentage let the maids do their job. Many Indians have commented that I have wasted my education and training by being a mom and homemaker. However, at an official party in the USA, my husband's colleagues actually gave me a standing ovation when I introduced myself as a mom and a homemaker.

Newspapers and media in India encourage women to think of their individuality outside the boundaries of home and family. Their identity is essentially tied up to how much outsiders praise them, even if their husbands and kids suffer. Agatha Christie, the empress of crime fiction, wrote in her autobiography that when women started coveting jobs outside and looking down on setting up homes, they exchanged their position from that of a queen to a slave!

Individuality is something you find within yourself, not with the help of the rest of the world. My biggest trophies are my sons and the pleasure I have in making a home for my husband all over the world. And believe me, that is a big challenge!

Take, for example, setting up home in China. You come across people who believe in TIC (This is China), and who compromise their own comforts and needs. There are also people who do not believe in TIC, like me, and who find ways of satisfying their own and their family's needs.

TIC is a phrase the expats use when they find they can't resolve their housing, transport, or purchase issues. Nowadays, even some of the enlightened Chinese housing or relocation agents use this abbreviation when they don't want to do a job or don't want to get it done. Basically, they ask you to compromise your standards. After seeing the fabulous opening of the Beijing Olympics and observing the contentment level and pride of the Chinese in the progress of their country, I concluded that TIC is a phrase that for the Chinese means NG (No Go). They do not see the need to serve you, though if you are adamant enough, you can still get it done.

We had some issues with one of our drivers, and I wanted him changed. Our relocation agency told me TIC. The agent was a Chinese. I told her that I would not take no for an answer. At the end of the week I had my new driver, and the woman had to swallow her words. Similarly, my dry-cleaning lady developed a respectful attitude toward me when I told her that I expected the curtains and venetian blinds to be fitted back perfectly after dry-cleaning despite her telling me TIC. I told her as a person from the country that could host the Olympics opening as they did, she did not have the right to say TIC. She was happy with my response, and she did my job perfectly. She continues as my dry-cleaning lady to this day.

After all, during the Beijing Olympics, they even managed to keep the clouds at bay. Isn't that almost playing God?

However, in China, most of the educated are free thinkers and do not believe in God!

Being in an international community in China, sometimes I come across unusual people or situations. I've been following the blog of a Dutch American family that has taken a year off to tour the Americas with their children in a mobile home. This family sold all their accumulated belongings of many years—something most of us would find difficult to do—bought a mobile home in the USA, and are driving around the whole of the Americas, homeschooling their two kids. The mom of the family was Surya's class teacher in grade one. It is fun to read about their adventures as they drive around the Americas. Before she left Suzhou, Surya's teacher told me that long ago, before having two kids, she and her husband backpacked through Vietnam and thought it was great fun! I admire this family for their courage. I am sure their kids are going to be richer for this experience. To reject the rat race for a year and then re-enter requires a phenomenal amount of guts and discipline. It gives you such a sense of exhilaration and freedom when you think you will wake up to a new place every morning!

Another person worth mentioning is the old man who helps me in the garden. To date, I do not know his name. He has been serving me with a smile for more than a year. He is sixty-five, has a headful of bristly white hair, and is always smiling. In the summers, every morning he comes and waters my garden, arriving around 7 a.m. He has a theory that because the ground grows hot in summers, the plants catch a cold if you water them later in the day. You have to water them early, before the ground becomes hot, or late, after the ground cools down. Did you ever hear or think of that one? Other people who attend to lot of expats' needs are home helpers, or *ayis*. Ayis from different areas of China have different characteristics. The ones from Xi'an and Sichuan are most sought-after, as they work hard and try to earn as much as possible for their families back home. I had an ayi from Xi'an for five years, and I really miss her. She could cook and clean really well! Also, she loved Indian and Italian food. She retired after the five years and went back to her homeland. She now has a big two-storey home and two gifted daughters with white-collar jobs who don't want their mother to do housekeeping for others. In China, if kids are gifted, the government makes sure they do well, as they did with my old ayi's daughters.

I did not much like the attitude of Sichuanese ayis, as the ones I came across valued only money and had no sense of loyalty to the home they worked for. Now I have a local Suzhounese ayi. She is a good, kind soul with a big heart. She is always smiling and quite hardworking. However, she can't cook for nuts. Her eyes water when she chops onions. She finds Indian and Italian food too spicy. For the few days that my old ayi trained her, there were regular kitchen conflicts between them. My Xi'an ayi would add more-than-usual chilli to the food, and my Suzhounese ayi would not be able to eat it! There was a regular battle on in the kitchen where my Suzhounese ayi came out with eyes streaming with water from dry chilli frying in oil. All the Chinese dishes I had asked my ayi from Xi'an to teach her went unlearnt, as the food was spicier than usual and the dry chilli fumes made my Suzhounese ayi water at the nose and eyes.

In Suzhou, they use sugar as a spice! The food that my current ayi cooks has salt, sugar, and oil. I have actually seen her add sugar instead of salt to a dish of sausages and potatoes that she was cooking for her lunch. And once she said she would eat homemade pizzas for lunch, just as we were doing. Then she told me the pizzas are tasty when sprinkled with a bit of sugar and rice (cooked the night before). I have never dared to taste her handiwork, and she has forgotten whatever cuisine my old ayi taught her. Well, I love cooking, so this is not really a big issue for me.

Though most expats would bunch the whole population as Chinese, each area in China has its own distinct culture, cuisine, and dialect, much as India does. However, the official written and spoken language is Mandarin. The spoken dialects have no written scripts. My ayi from Xi'an always looked down her nose at the Suzhounese dialect and culture, especially the food! I had to learn a few Suzhounese turns, twists, and words to be able to communicate with my current ayi. She admits Aditya speaks better Mandarin than her! She can speak the local dialect to perfection, which is a big help, because when I have local repairmen in the house, she knows exactly how to handle them. My Xi'an ayi was misled by the local workers, and she just could not deal with them! Sometimes she could not understand their language.

When we came to China, like most companies, my husband's company encouraged us to pick up Mandarin. I had a university student coming home to teach me. Then I asked her for certain phrases to talk to my Xi'an ayi. The Mandarin she taught me was so pure that my ayi from Xi'an could not understand the words. I took my tutor to a local stationery store for a practical lesson. I found the shopkeeper did not understand her at all. My teacher said they spoke impure Mandarin laced with local dialect, so she could not speak to them. We managed with body language, which is pretty much what I used all the time initially.

Language is a means to communicate. I needed Chinese to communicate with my ayi, driver, shopkeepers, and so forth. I did not want to be a Mandarin scholar. So I was happy and relieved when my tutor informed me that my class timings clashed with her university schedule. I was more than happy to let her go. When she volunteered her friend for teaching me, I asked her to give me the contact details and said that I would get in touch with the friend later, after a break. Almost five and a half years have passed, and my break has not yet ended!

Now I can speak to my ayi, driver, gardener, and storekeepers. They assure me my Mandarin is very good. And my bilingual

Chinese friends assure me that my Mandarin is very low-class. One of them told me I speak Mandarin like a maid! Her comment sounded like what Henry Higgins would call "verbal class distinction" in an essentially communist society!

Pearl S. Buck's novel *The Good Earth* touches upon the divide between the northern and southern cultures. And believe me, living six years in China I have discovered difference in values and culture among people from different regions of China. I have seen a Shanghainese sneer at a Suzhounese. Taxi drivers in Beijing say that the food in Suzhou is unpalatable. Mind you, food in Beijing is absolutely fabulous, especially their mutton. Of course, you do get things on the roadside, like scorpions on the skewer, which we have never had the guts to try!

To ignore the differences between different distinctive cultures in China and India is like asking a Finn to forget his own culture and to adapt the Italian or German or Polish culture as an unified European culture.

Getting back to a topic that always delights me: food—there is no distinctive thing known as Chinese food in China. There is no generic cuisine, again much as in India. Every local culture has a distinct cuisine and strong likes and dislikes. You do not get chop suey or chow mein in China of the type we know in India or the USA. Each region has a distinct way of cooking. The quality of rice differs. There are staunch Buddhist vegetarians. There are avid meat eaters.

I personally prefer the cuisine in Beijing, Chengdu, Xinjiang, and Hong Kong. In Beijing, other than the famous Beijing duck, which you eat with a salad and a thin crepe, you get fabulous mutton. Donkey's meat and grilled scorpion are dishes I have never been able to try. In Chengdu, I can't recall exactly what I ate, but I remember I enjoyed the local cuisine. Aditya went to clean panda cages near Chengdu with nine more boys and two male teachers, and said that he enjoyed the local cuisine and ate a delicious dish of fish and tofu laced with caterpillars. Well, I had no temptation ever to try any kind of worms, including Guilin specialties, like silkworm noodles and wine laced with snake.

I had a brush with Xinjiang cuisine on my flight back from Xi'an. There is a big Muslim community in Xi'an, and it is said many of them are from Xinjiang. They gave us a kind of burger with some fantastic meat preparation inside. Now we indulge our palate for Xinjiang food in a couple of restaurants near our home. They make delicious barbecued lamb, stuff similar to lamb burgers, and cheese-free lamb pizzas, lamb curries, and breads. Aditya chose one of these restaurants to celebrate his outstanding grade-ten results over and above a five-star hotel because the food made him drool!

In Xi'an the food is spicy but a trifle too oily for our taste. My Xi'an lady learnt to cook with less oil, and that was tasty. She claimed what she made often was Cantonese as she had been trained in Cantonese cuisine by her former boss. She never quite managed to pick up Indian or Italian cuisine.

She could never brown the onions right for Indian food, and she mixed up Indian and Italian spices, since I have them both on the rack. Once I found her flavouring the dal with oregano instead of cumin and then I decided I could not afford the risk of teaching her Indian cuisine. The spices in my house are labelled in English, and I do not know their Chinese names.

Cantonese food, or food from Hong Kong, is delicious. I love their steamed fish, fried chicken, dim sums with shrimp and pork, fried rice with egg white, and some strange green vegetable. I asked my old ayi to make the fried rice, but she said she did not know how to.

However, I had an amazing adventure with chow mein when I was new to Suzhou. My husband was travelling, so I decided to take a day off cooking. I told my ayi to make chow mein, a popular dish with both my kids and me. She told me she needed sausages and a special noodle. I took her shopping. She bought some kind of small spinach and thick noodles which were pre-cooked. At home, she dipped the noodles in hot water and then sautéed them in a lot of oil with sliced sausage and the spinach. It was very oily and difficult to eat. But that was her chow mein and not what we are used to eating in India or the USA.

Sometimes someone asks me if I can make Indian chicken curry. Every state in India has a different, distinctive preparation of chicken curry, and some of them have a variety of chicken curries, so what is it you dish? India has over two hundred dialects and distinct cultures. Out of these, many are vegetarian and many are non-vegetarian. Each non-vegetarian culture has a number of preparations of chicken curry. So which one would I make? In China, it is much the same.

A couple of months after we came to China, we were exploring different foods. Once we saw a restaurant that said it offered Sichuan food. We mistook it for Schezwuan or Hong Kong cuisine and went in. We ordered some chicken and we discovered it was a cold dish with some kind of oily preserve. Then we asked for a hot chicken dish. They showed us a soup. We agreed, but it turned out to be a chicken organ soup with no meat in it! The next day I was swollen with urticaria. I could not open my eyes and had to be rushed to the hospital. The doctor said that the allergy started from my digestive system, and she gave me a ten-minute slow shot. My husband took leave that day . . . and all for our attempts to explore Chinese food, like a bunch of provincial foreigners!

Once a friend of mine and I went to try the local cuisine in Suzhou. I ordered chilli chicken and she ordered barbecue sausages. When the food arrived, I was unhappy, as I could only see huge pieces of garlic, a few dried chillies, and no chicken! Then I found tiny bits of chicken under the garlic. It was amazing! What would I eat with the rice? I could not eat garlic or chilli and no chicken with rice only! My friend took a bite of the barbecued sausages and pushed it away. "Too sweet," she said. I had eaten sweetish Taiwanese sausages in Singapore. So I tried one and almost puked. It was like sugar instead of salt in the sausage.

One of the things I love to eat in Jiangsu is a kind of pancake with different toppings on it. These are mixed with the batter when the pancake is fried. It is really scrumptious. It is of course not Suzhounese in origin.

There are regions in Jiangsu that like spicy food. I discovered that my gardener loves chillies. He lives a few hours drive from Suzhou. One day we had a funny experience. My gardener thanked my Suzhounese ayi for handing him some gardening tools from the garage. She jokingly told him that he would have to treat her to a meal to thank her properly. When she laughingly told me how she managed to wrangle a treat out of the old man, I said that was funny because he ate hot, spicy food, and she would be weeping and feeling indisposed at the end of the meal because she could not tolerate even the smell of spicy food. Promptly, she ran to the window, opened it, and shouted out to him that she was joking and did not expect a treat from him!

One of the things we discovered on coming to China is that even Singaporean Chinese cuisine, which claims to be traditional Chinese, is much different from the real stuff. One of our favourite dishes is Haianese chicken rice. In Singapore, you get steamed or roasted chicken with a delicious sauce of ginger and chillies. Sometimes they even give you some spinach on the side and always sliced cucumbers. You can have the chicken boneless or with bones. In China we discovered that when we asked for chicken rice there were no options. We were given mainly chicken skin and bone with a little bit of undercooked meat hanging on it, lots of oily spinach and cucumber, and none of the tasty chilli sauce.

The other interesting thing that has evolved in Suzhou is *fusion* cuisine—Western food adapted to local ingredients. Pizza Hut here has a lot of that. Some of it is not so bad, and some of it is uneatable, as it is too oily and sweet, and the cheese always tastes the same: papery, oily, and strange!

Once we went for fusion Thai cuisine. Their chilli crab was not bad, and they had a very nice tom yum soup with pork dumplings. Different but nice!

The strangest result of fusion cuisine was seen in a cake. We were having a Diwali cum birthday lunch at my house for some of my husband's office colleagues who live wifeless in Suzhou. Their wives have careers and therefore need to shuttle between the country where they work and China. One of our guests felt too embarrassed to come without a gift in hand. He brought cake, as that seemed closest to Diwali sweets. It was a blueberry jam cake. I would say good cake, except there was too much cream icing and cherry tomatoes and celery leaves on top for dressing. These were even glazed with sugar! Officially, tomato is a fruit, but the celery leaves? In China I took to baking my own stuff, as I found that cakes and cookies are not always to our taste. Once we had a lovely gingerbread house which used yellow ginger or turmeric instead of normal ginger. Of course, we realized that the house was beautiful only to look at and not likely to give us gastronomical delight after taking a bite. The cakes in local shops here invariably have too much cream.

The Indian restaurants here are sometimes truly Indian and sometimes fusion. Getting vegetarian Western food is a challenge, though I know there is a vegetarian Chinese restaurant. I had never had the urge to savour it, as the cleanliness level seemed a little compromised. Finally my husband convinced me that his American colleagues recommended the restaurant. One day when we were lunching together without our kids, we went in. The funny thing was they had no hot tea, only free coffee after lunch. The food was too bland for my palate. And I don't want to repeat my tryst with vegetarianism in that restaurant ever again.

One needs to watch out for the cleanliness standards while eating out in China. You also have to make sure that the restaurants provide serving spoons or chopsticks with every dish because the Chinese just pick the food from the serving dish with the chopsticks they put in their mouths. Lots of foreigners try to humour this practice. But like all bad practices, this should be done away with. It encourages the spread of germs and diseases from one person to another. My Xi'an ayi told me that a lot of people would be offended that I was so picky about serving spoons. I told her it doesn't matter, as I don't want to compromise a good practice for a bad one! I still need serving spoons wherever I go!

CHAPTER 10

Sporting Matters

SPORTS ARE A MAJOR preoccupation in the expat community.

In the month of May, you have the Dragon Boat Race, which centres around a two-thousand-year-old legend of a poet named Qu Yuan. The patriotic poet jumped into the waters of the Yangtze when his country was occupied by the state of Qin. People were greatly distressed and threw dumplings and eggs into the river to prevent the fish from getting at his body. The annual Dragon Boat Races commemorate the death anniversary of Qu Yuan. They race boats made to look like dragons. The expat community participates in a major way. Expat women exercise and practice round the year for these races. Boats and teams sponsored by different countries race down the lakes in Suzhou. It is a colourful event.

More mundane sports like football, tennis, basketball, hockey, and volleyball also have some amount of fan following. Football is the game that fascinates many in our family . . . my sons, their dad, their uncle, and others. When he was young, my husband broke his jaw playing football, my brother-in-law his nose, my cousin's son his shoes. So when my eight-year-old told me with determination that he wanted to go for the football team trials, I was not too excited. He has been playing football in the school soccer club every Saturday morning for the past two years. I have not been thrilled to bits about it but quite tolerant, as he needs to let off his excess energy.

But trying for the under-nine team is another matter. They play matches and have a team manager, whose picture with panda poop in his hand is on my iPad. The reason I have his picture is because he was one of the teachers who accompanied Aditya to the panda reserve to clean panda cages in Chengdu. So when he decided to bark at the prospectives after the trial, I showed his panda-poop picture to all the moms. I have also seen him blow his nose on the football field. Another coach once spat on the field. None of this seems sanitary or well-behaved to me. When I tried complaining to Aditya's principal, who was coordinating the Saturday morning football, he smiled and said in a most insincere tone, "Oh, did he? I will have a word with him about it."

When I complained to my husband, he said, "What? You complained about it? You must be crazy. Where did you expect him to spit?"

It looks like if you play football, you are welcome not to have a handkerchief or a tissue, to be dirty, and to forget all hygienic practices and good manners.

Aditya's principal also swears by my eight-year-old's goalkeeping. I feel proud that he plays well, but I also feel apprehensive. When I say he needs protective gear, they point to his shin pads and gloves. I want him to add a shield for the body and a helmet with a face covering to his gear. Everyone laughs at me when I say this.

Aditya says, "Mamma, that is only for American football and that is not football at all."

Well, when Aditya plays football, he kicks his shoe up in the air along with the ball!

Aditya is the blue-eyed boy of all his teachers. He loves studying. So when I mentioned this fact to his vice-principal, he said, "Oh! Then Aditya plays like me!" Maybe there is still hope for Aditya because I hear his vice-principal is a good player. Or was his vice-principal merely covering up?

Aditya and his friends took up boxing. Meanwhile, I heard a girl could knock them down . . . she was that good!

Sports are not Aditya's strong point, but he is sporting by nature and can laugh at his own shortcomings. However, Aditya's general knowledge about sports is excellent. Mine wasn't. I was not only bad at sports but also was disinterested in any news about sports. I used to hide behind library shelves and pretend to arrange books during physical education classes in school. I used to read the books on the shelves and start dusting when the teacher came, so the shelves took ever so long to arrange. And I had to keep at it with the teacher signing me off for PE.

My husband, on the other hand, actually liked cricket and football. He played them and watched them. Once I was mad at my brother-in-law for erasing a movie I had recorded (in the days of VCRs—video cassette recorders) by recording a football match on top of it! He and my husband watched the match!

Football is in my younger son's blood, I decided after watching him play. He is a good goalie, and once in a while I see him make a fabulous goal, too. He really enjoys the game. While my elder son's principal keeps praising his baby brother's goalkeeping skills, I think of the tiny solid body being assailed with footballs. In the last match, one boy jumped over his ears in an attempt to kick the ball out of his grip. He was not too good with his aim. Therefore, he did not injure my son. But even if a player is given a yellow or red or purple card and thrown out of the game, he can still hurt my little one badly. As I mentioned, my husband broke his jaw when one of his friends tried to give a header. My brother-in-law broke his nose trying to save a goal. I do not want my little one injured by anyone.

But one good thing about football is that Surya is learning to tie his shoelaces on his own, unlike his elder brother, who ties them in knots and claims that his shoelace cannot be opened by all and sundry.

Tying shoelaces brings to mind ties that complicate life eternally in my household. I don't mean emotional ties or ties of relationships; I refer to the simple thing called neckties.

Before I married, I had seen my grandfather, father, and uncle equally at ease with Bengali dhotis (a five-metre length of cloth which men wrap around themselves instead of trousers) and

Western formalwear. They could wear dhotis and ties and cravats immaculately. So imagine my surprise when I found my husband and brother-in-law having trouble with dhotis . . . which became undone, much to their embarrassment. My brother-in-law could manage ties and cravats well enough. My husband extended his inability to manage dhotis to any kind of tied formalwear. Aditya, who is now sixteen, has added to this an inability to tie shoelaces. Surya is learning to tie his laces perfectly, because it's difficult for him to exit a game to tie his shoelaces.

I think part of the reason my brother-in-law manages to tie his neckties well is that he went into sales and now runs a company in South Africa. My husband is quintessentially a researcher. He does sums and generates ideas for a living. Most people listen to him because he says things which only he can say. Unfortunately, in today's world, even if you are a top-notch researcher, you have to manage huge teams, and if your ideas are considered outstanding, you have to present and need to dress formally. My husband has had the distinction of visiting formal meetings in jeans. When he had to go on an official visit to Boston, I told him to take a suit. He said, "If they want my expertise, they will be willing to listen to me if I am in shorts!" He went in jeans. He did his work, came back, and admitted everyone was in a suit except him and he felt out of place.

Then there was the time he had to give a series of lectures in different places in China. He had been asked to wear a tie. The flight to Shenzhen was delayed due to bad weather. The air hostesses had to dance to appease irritated Chinese flyers. The flight reached in time for the reception, where my husband was the chief speaker. He went in jeans and delivered his speech to an astounding round of international applause again.

However, now has come a time when he, as part of the management team, needs to go to functions as a VIP. He has a real problem because if he does not dress well, he will offend local people who are reporting to him or to others like him! In China, dressing is a serious business. People customarily overdress. A neighbor once commented my Chinese maid dressed better than me on an average day. "That is why she is my maid!" I responded. She comes to work, takes her work seriously, and therefore dresses nicely. While I am forgiven dressing lapses as an eccentric foreigner, my husband cannot afford that. He needs to dress well, with a tie and a suit and sometimes a boutonnière. He hates it. I love it. I think he looks like a lost schoolboy when he dresses formally.

Aditya has inherited his father's inability to dress formally. He wears black and grey and grey and black. So when he has to deliver a speech and wear a tie and suit, he normally remembers to tell me at bedtime. I get frantic and angry. I iron his shirt. Sometimes, if his coat has grown small, I need to improvise. God alone knows how I would have managed one time, if it had not been for my father's Harris tweed, which he had gifted to his grandson and is a bit big for him. So at least he can wear it—unlike his own coat, which comes halfway to his elbow and his waist.

Then there is the problem of ties. The only tie my son wears is one with a picture of a lion against the sun. Anything else, he claims, is too shiny for him. Aditya's tie reminds me of *The Lion King*. The backdrop is black and the pictures on it are overbright, in hues of orange, yellow, and red. It was given to him by his eighth-grade humanities teacher, who wrote a beautiful piece on their class as his parting gift (as he visualized them thirty years down the line). He described my son as a Lucasian Professor who wore his pants inside out and tried to concoct mathematical formulas to slow down the revolutions of the earth! He thought my son, brilliant, and the tie was a parting blessing to him. So his student considers it necessary to wear it on every occasion that demands a tie. It's like a signature tune.

Of course, I need to knot the tie. If it comes undone, he needs help!

His father can claim the distinction of tying the tie with the help of a download on his Galaxy tablet. The download gives visual and textual step-by-step instructions on how to knot a tie! To make his task easier, I knot it for him. But finding a tie is an issue for him. He always misplaces what I buy. Then if he leaves the knot on, it crumples. So when he wants to reuse the tie, he needs to iron it himself, as it is always the last minute. And then he burns it!

One time I had to buy him a tie, knot it, and send it over with our chauffeur while he was at work in the morning, so that he could use it in the afternoon. The night before, he burnt his only available decent tie when he tried to iron it around 11.45 p.m. Aditya needed his Lion King tie and formal outfit for giving a speech at school that morning, too. He informed me at 7 p.m. that twelve hours later he would be donning a suit to go to school and give a speech. That he had outgrown his formal suit and tailors are not available at midnight was a non-issue for him. That is the time I said many thanks to my dad, who gave him his treasured coat.

I had just got over with this formalwear episode when my husband's started. He needed his formals by 11 a.m. the same day. His ties were unavailable for various reasons, like being lost, burnt, and so on. My son's function was over at 9.30 a.m. My husband, tieless, needed something by 11 a.m. I dropped my husband off to work, went and shopped for groceries and a tie, knotted it, and sent it with my chauffeur by 10.30 a.m.

That is how trying tying ties can be in our household!

CHAPTER 11

Culture Shock

WHENEVER FOREIGNERS COME TO China, they experience culture shock! There are certain things in China which aren't found elsewhere, like doorless public toilets.

Speaking of toilets, my mother-in-law found her expectations were belied. We went to eat at what seemed to be a high-quality Hong Kong restaurant beside the canal. My mother-in-law wanted to use the washroom. I asked them where the washroom was. They said, "*Mei you.*" "Don't have," I translated for my mother-in-law. She did not want to believe it. She asked me to ask again in Chinese. They said, "*Mei you.*" I translated, explaining that they don't have a bathroom in the restaurant. I said if she was desperate, we could go to the mall. No. She was not desperate, but she found it hard to believe. Every country she had visited has restaurants with bathrooms. She had been to Singapore, Malaysia, South Africa, and China, and she lived in many places in India. This was a new experience for her. She made me ask for the non-existent bathroom five times. And she made sure I asked five different waiters. She could not believe me. After the meal, when we were leaving, she wanted to explore the second level of the restaurant to look for a bathroom.

"You probably didn't ask correctly" was her verdict. I was truly embarrassed. I rushed her out and took her to the neighbouring mall, which had clean, modern, proper toilets with doors! China is essentially a mix of old and new cultures. Part of this can be seen in the choice of cultural performances that often dot the streets of the town centre or parks. The most astounding was in the park of the Temple of Heaven. On one side, we had hip line dancing and on the other music with traditional erhu and somebody practicing tai chi, a form of Chinese exercise, which is performed slowly to music. What is important is that all of this seems to harmonize together.

In Chengdu, we heard some fabulous singing on the roadside from old folks. Their movements suggested what they were doing was traditional. The harmonization of old and new, of traditional and modern is astounding in China.

A seemingly modern Chinese, one who calls himself a free thinker, still feels the need of parental approval for major things like jobs, relocation, and marriage. They also have rituals at death, Chinese New Year, and the May 1 and October 1 holidays, which they follow like a religion. The modern educated Chinese see themselves as free thinkers, but during the four occasions I have listed, China moves out to celebrate. Their traditional holidays have nothing to do with the rest of the world's religions. They do not give holidays on Christmas, Diwali, Id, or any other occasions that involve any world religions. All their holidays are essentially secular, though people observe them ritualistically like a religion. They go out. Trains and flights are overbooked. Hotels are jam-packed. Restaurants, especially the big Chinese ones, are overflowing. People are having a good time. When the holidays finish, they get back to work.

It is a systematic society that moves within a given framework of suits and ties.

The other thing that hassles foreigners is often the language barrier. They have opened many schools to teach foreigners Chinese. Unfortunately, most of these schools focus on the official Mandarin language. In China, each region has its own dialect. Where I live, they speak Suzhounese, which sounds like a series of z's. The local population, especially the older people, do not understand, read, write, or speak Mandarin. When I speak to my gardener, he partially understands me. My driver has to manage the dialect to explain things to him. At every bend of daily life, one finds linguistic challenges that need to be sorted out. Also, even when a foreigner speaks in Chinese, a lot of people are so stupefied that they do not make an effort to understand. There are also complex accents. *Wen* (pronounced as "one") means "to ask." The same word pronounced as "wo-un" means to kiss. So you really need to be careful with your accents!

One of the things I miss most in China is bookstores with English books. They are few in number. Normally, Xinghua, a big Chinese bookstore chain, has a floor devoted to foreign books, most of them in English. There are some foreign-goods stores that stock hot-selling books. Beijing offers a little variety . . . if you can call it that. Shanghai has one good bookstore. In Suzhou, bookstores are almost non-existent. They have a few attempts at foreign bookstores, but they are dirty, inadequate, and hideously overpriced. And if you are into downloading books, you could face issues because the Internet can be heavily monitored and slow.

Television channels legally are all in Chinese, except for CCTV 9, which relays some English programmes. We do get satellite TV. The landlords get it for foreigners, but it is not really allowed, agents say. So, satellite TV is largely intermittent. It comes smoothly for a while and goes. It can go for a number of reasons, including what can be perceived as a threat to China. However, I have also heard that legal satellite TV exists in China but is allowed only in hotels and educational institutions.

Housing is another issue that always confuses the newcomer to China.

I have seen housing in India. I have seen housing in England. I have seen housing in Holland. I have seen housing in Norway. I have seen housing in Singapore. I have seen housing in America. And now I am seeing housing in China.

China, with its huge population, has resolved a large part of its housing issues. Most of the local population have houses to live in. In towns like Suzhou, where I live, a large area is being developed to house the rich and expatriates. These houses are far bigger and cater to the luxurious tastes of the rich and not famous. Some of the things I have come across while house-hunting among such compounds left me breathless.

I had heard of gold-plated toilets in Hong Kong, but here I came across a house with a musical toilet bowl. The toilet seat sang and opened and closed every time you walked past! It is like the toilet seat is waving at you and inviting you to sit on it. The house I live in now thankfully does not have this feature. Instead, it has a musical washing machine that sings when the clothes are done; a fridge that, if left open for a little long, starts to play a tune; and a microwave that turns musical to indicate it has completed its job. The local population must be fond of tunes. However, it took me awhile to live with this high-tech music, and unfortunately, I have yet to develop an appreciation for it.

Another house I saw had a high-tech computer-controlled flushing system that I never had the guts to explore. Then there was a house with a huge bathtub that had an attached TV. Or was it a computer screen? This house also had a toilet for men and a separate one for women downstairs. I never quite figured out why! They were like public toilets.

Another peculiar thing that seems to be gaining popularity here is high-tech front doors. They are computerized doors. Unfortunately, sometimes they do not work. My husband and I once went to see a house where the front door couldn't be unlocked because the computer was malfunctioning. The agent took us in by the back door. Luckily, my current house is devoid of this feature. However, we did live in a flat for two years with a high-tech back door that got jammed at first. Then when they opened it, they couldn't close it. They said we were not using the door properly. It was the first time I heard that you needed training to open and close a door, and I was forty-three! I still do not understand why we need to complicate our already complex lives with such high-tech doorways! Finally, after much ado, it did get fixed properly.

There are sensitive lights that turn on when they sense your presence. However, they turn off as soon as you stop moving. So when you stand under such a light, you have to keep prancing around to make your presence felt! Most of these lights are located in the common dark area of exclusive estates. It feels a bit peculiar when you have to keep doing a hornpipe in front of your friend's flat till he or she opens the door. You just hope their neighbours will not come out and see you doing your jig.

I have seen houses with fourteen or more rooms, counting from the basement. They are bizarre and big. The house with the computer-screen bathtub had a room within a room within a room. It was unbelievable that designs could be so complicated.

In Suzhou, whenever they talk about European housing, you have to understand it's tall and narrow, most likely with four levels, and staircases that do not take children's safety into consideration. The American-style houses are similar, and the Chinese-style houses have closets within bathrooms within rooms within rooms. The garages, often sloping and at basement level, are flooded during heavy downpours of rain.

One of the most essential things in China is to find a house with a good landlord. Agents can be changed if you can talk to a landlord directly. Many of them are educated and can understand and speak English. They are just too shy to try it on a foreigner. You have to be friendly and kind for them to trust you enough to try their first English sentence.

Good landlords often install all the equipment and floor or wall heating for you. The catch is when winter starts, the government normally rations gas. In a lot of the houses, gas runs the heating. So if you run out of gas, you run out of hot water and heating when it is snowing outside. If you take a house that uses electricity to run all this equipment, the bill you tote up in a couple of months can well be over 10,000 RMB.

Many of the compounds boast swimming pools.

We were staying in a compound that boasted two pools—only one didn't function. One was on the first level, and the lifeguard at the functional pool said the other one's pump malfunctioned. The pool, which we used, was strange. There were almost no markings, and they used lots of powdered chlorine, which kind of hurt your bare feet when it touched the bottom, where the powder lay undissolved. Maybe they did this to force us to swim! Lazy people like me would be forced to lose their layers of blubber.

There was a spa, which doubled up as the kids' pool, but the water seemed thick and unclean. However, in winter, when the pools are empty and house agents show you the flats for rent, they always indicate that there are two pools and a spa in that compound. How much of the pool is functional and clean is another matter which you need to look into.

Agents the world over try to sell you anything that can earn them a living. I am not against agents. But one thing I know: people become agents to make big money. Serving their client well may or may not be a priority. If serving you is your agent's priority, you are lucky.

Then there was the pool in the compound next to ours. My sons visited the pools with their friends. And they came back saying that the design, with its water slide, was fabulous—but the pool was unusable because they forgot to make drains. So now the pool is filled with dirty rainwater and scum. The only creatures swimming in it are the mud skidders and frogs and insects. It is probably the best breeding ground for mosquitoes here! But it is still officially a swimming pool, albeit one that doesn't function.

My brave swimmers came back without attempting to swim at the pool. My six-year-old, however, was a little wet. He said that he had slipped and fallen on the slime of the pool's stairs while he and his eight-year-old friend were escaping from a ghost that haunted the pool. His eight-year-old friend is right in a way to propound the theory of the mythical spirit. It is, after all, a ghost pool, much in the line of a ghost town—abandoned and derelict!

In yet another compound in China, where again only one pool is functional, you had pet doggies bathing in the outdoor wading pool for children, so the pool was drained and closed down!

Our first compound in China had a comparatively nice indoor pool, though the pool's rooftop rained water when the water condensed on it in summers. And that was tough for me, as I float with my face up toward the ceiling. *Plop*, went a water drop, dirty ceiling water near my mouth! Other than this, I almost liked the pool. They had a baby wading pool, a one-metre pool with a water slide, a full-sized pool, and a spa. The spa was unused most of the time and never looked very clean, but nothing like our neighbouring compound's ghost pool. We and our friends had a lot of fun in the pool that rained condensed water.

You need to be above cultural differences if you want to enjoy China. You have to see them in a historical context to figure out Chinese thought processes. The Chinese came from a culture that was deeply deprived and exploited by the rich and powerful. China had no sense of democracy for centuries. Then came the teacher Mao. He made changes starting in the 1950s. Then came the opening up, and then a flood of foreigners with strange customs, bringing money and many lucrative jobs for the sons of Han. China has moved at a breakneck speed since the 1950s. Once a population of have-nots, they have become a huge consumerist population of haves—who love to shop, dress up, party, and catch up on all the fun and money they missed out on over the centuries of toil and the building of the Great Wall.

One fantastic thing about living in China is its vastly different kinds of vegetation and insect population. It has enormous insects, huge, and with daring colours. The worms that I find in my garden are fat and green. Something you avoid doing is using Chinese pesticides, when you don't know what they are. At a nursery they told me to get rid of bugs by cutting off the infested area of the plants. In any case, once it gets colder, the bugs die on their own.

The local vegetation consists of gorgeous flowers and unusual leafy plants. Their peonies are lush and pink and stay for a long time. The osmanthus flowers perfume the air. *Avatar*, the movie, evidently drew inspiration from landscapes in China.

Plants are sometimes imported from Japan. In spring, our compounds turn pink with cherry blossoms. The hedges turn yellow or pink with blossoms. It's wonderful. I have plants near my pond that turn mauve every summer. Their flowers are lovely.

China is unique, but it is as you make it.

If you want, you can find things to make you feel happy and smile, and if you wish, you can frown all the while!

Take it or leave it.

CONCLUSION

WHEN MY HUSBAND AND I left India in 1991, we boarded the flight to Singapore with two suitcases and a bag. We planned to be back in two years. The two years have stretched to over twenty, and now, even when I travel for two weeks with my family, which has doubled its numbers, I need four suitcases, four backpacks, and cabin luggage. I do not know when we will return, but I do know that I am richer for all the experiences I have had over the years. My children are fortunate to have friends from all over the world and a wide variety of experiences. Every day I thank God for the blessings he has showered on us and for the fantastic future which is sure to unfurl before us.

Printed in the United States
By Bookmasters